· CONCISE GUIDE TO ·

Tendon and Ligament Injuries
in the Horse

Also by David W. Ramey, D.V.M.

Horsefeathers: Facts Versus Myths About Your Horse's Health

Concise Guide to Medications and Supplements for the Horse

Concise Guide to Colic in the Horse

Concise Guide to Navicular Syndrome in the Horse

· CONCISE GUIDE TO ·

Tendon and Ligament Injuries in the Horse

David W. Ramey, D.V.M.

Howell Book House
New York

Howell Book House
A Simon & Schuster Macmillan Company
1633 Broadway
New York, NY 10019

MACMILLAN is a registered trademark of Macmillan, Inc.

Library of Congress Cataloging-in-Publication Data

Ramey, David W.
        Concise guide to tendon and ligament injuries in the
horse/David W. Ramey.
                p.   cm.
        Includes bibliographical references and index.
        ISBN 0-87605-912-4
        I. Tendons—Wounds and injuries.
2. Ligaments—Wounds and injuries.   3. Horses—Wounds and
injuries.   I. Title.
SF959.T47R35 1996   95-25005
636.1'0897474044—dc20   CIP

Manufactured in the United States of America

10 9 8 7 6 5 4 3 2 1

Contents

ACKNOWLEDGMENTS

As ever, this book is the end result of a lot of help. Trying to distill medical jargon into terms that can be understood by people without a medical education can be a bit challenging. Unfortunately, sometimes the author wasn't quite up to the challenge.

Fortunately, that's where the help comes in. Jonna Lee Pangburn creates beautiful art but also spends time in a world full of criticism; her criticisms here were a welcome and helpful addition. Denise Leeper, my new secretary (farewell, Sandra), found time between all the various duties of running my practice to put in her valuable two cents. Linda Rarey, intrepid crime fighter, invested not only time, but a fortune in "Post-It" notes to help bring the book into a level of understanding. Finally, Lynda Fenneman's wonderful illustrations once again give readers an idea of "what goes where." Thank you all.

INTRODUCTION

Tendon and ligament injuries represent one of the major problems facing the athletic horse. The tendons and ligaments of the lower limbs of the horse are very important structures for normal athletic movement. Unfortunately, they are also among the most commonly injured areas of the horse. An injury to a horse's tendons and ligaments can range from a minor, nagging problem to a severe, career-ending (or even life-ending) situation.

Many interesting observations as to the causes and treatment of these injuries have been made, but so far no one has been able always to prevent them from occurring. Nor has anyone been able to figure out a way to return the injured tissue to a normal, pre-injured state. Work is ongoing.

Tendon and ligament injuries are frustrating things to deal with in horses. The best way to deal with them would be to prevent them; unfortunately, some injuries are inevitable in any athlete. Once they have occurred, proper treatment can help minimize damage; a return to the pre-injured normal state is a goal that cannot be attained. Proper rehabilitation can help make sure that the horse will ultimately recover to the best degree possible.

The most extensively studied and most problematic tendons and ligaments in the horse are in the lower limbs. Consequently, most of this book is devoted to discussions of these areas. It begins with an overview of the anatomy and physiology of the major tendons and ligaments of the lower fore and hind limbs. It provides some general guidelines for proper treatment of the injured horse so that he can ultimately return to an athletic function. It discusses the many choices that must be made by the horse owner when faced with an injury to a tendon or a ligament. Ideally, it will help you know what to expect if your horse sustains such an injury. It will help you make an informed decision as to your horse's care. Knowledge is power.

CHAPTER I

The Major Tendons and Ligaments of the Foreleg and Hind Leg

ANATOMY IS A NECESSARY PART OF ANY DISCUSSION OF injuries to the horse's legs. After all, you can't expect to know how to deal with injured tissue unless you know where the injured tissue is or what it does. Fortunately, anatomically, tendons and ligaments are pretty simple.

Of course, tendons and ligaments exist all over the horse's body. However, the tendons and ligaments of the horse that are most prone to injury (and easiest to examine and treat) are in the lower legs. Those are the ones that are addressed in this book. In the forelimb, they are most obvious below the horse's knee (carpus). In the hind limb, they are easily seen and felt below the horse's hock (tarsus).

TENDONS

By definition, a tendon is a structure that connects a muscle to a bone. "Muscle" is the name that is given to one of the largest organs in the body. This organ does one thing: it contracts. When muscle contracts, it shortens its overall length. By contracting, the muscles of the musculo-skeletal system produce the movements of the horse's body via the horse's skeleton.

The skeleton is the framework that the horse's body is built upon. It is made up of over two hundred individual bones! Anywhere two bones meet is called a joint.

When a muscle contracts, bones of the skeleton move in relation to each other. This is accomplished by bending or moving bones around a joint. The pulling action of the muscles is accomplished via the various tendons. Think of your own arm. When the biceps muscle in your own arm contracts, the bones of the upper and lower arm are pulled closer together around the elbow joint. Thus, one of the important functions of tendons is to help transmit the force of the muscles to the bones. The muscle action that is exerted on the bones via the tendons causes the bones either to extend or to flex.

Extension describes the action of the horse's leg as it reaches forward to cover the ground. You can extend your own wrist by bending it back up towards your elbow. Tendons that connect the muscles responsible for muscular extension of the limbs to the bones are called, predictably, extensor tendons.

Flexion describes the action of the horse's limb as it bends up under his body. You can flex your finger by bending it towards your palm. Tendons that connect the muscles responsible for muscular flexion of the limbs to the bones are called—you guessed it—flexor tendons.

The tendon itself is constructed very much like a rope or a cable. It is one big cord made up of a lot of little fibers. In a tendon, these fibers run next to each other in a very organized, parallel fashion. The fibers are also cross-linked to each other from side to side. This parallel, cross-linked fiber arrangement gives the tendons tremendous strength and toughness in their own right. The inherent strength of the tendons is also very useful in stabilizing and supporting the various joints of the lower limb. This stabilizing and supporting of the limb represents a second very important function of tendons.

Even though they are parallel, tendon fibers aren't straight. Each of the tendon fibers has a little crimp in it. The crimp actually makes the tendon fibers look a bit wavy when they are examined under a microscope. It's thought that the crimped fiber arrangement of a tendon helps allow for the tendon to stretch. When pressure is applied to the tendon and then released, such as occurs when the horse bears weight on the leg, the little crimped fibers straighten out. They then return to their normal, wavy shape when the leg comes off the ground. Thus, a tendon is slightly elastic, in some ways like a rubber band. This elasticity means that the tendon can act as a shock absorber for the horse's legs.

Shock absorption is the third important function of a tendon. When a horse gallops, the tendons stretch out, almost to the point of breaking, when weight is put on the leg. They then snap back like bungee cords when the leg is lifted off the ground (this recoil also helps to return the limb to its starting position, a fourth important function of tendons). The stretching and giving of the tendon helps absorb the stresses and shock on the legs caused by the movement of the great weight of the horse.

LIGAMENTS

A ligament, by definition, is a band of fibrous tissue that acts as a supporting structure. Unlike tendons, ligaments don't have any role in the active muscle movements of the horse's body. Instead, they are important stabilizers of the horse's musculoskeletal system. Ligaments keep bones, tendons and muscles from stretching or moving too much in relation to each other. For example, say you put one bone on top of another one, such as is seen in the horse's fetlock joint. Obviously, the bones aren't going to just sit in place when the horse starts to move unless something is there to hold them in place. The horse's body has been designed so that firm, fibrous straps are placed all around the joint, attached to both of its sides, so that the bones can't slide off to the side or otherwise get out of place. These straps are called ligaments.

Ligaments are generally described in terms of their location and function. For example, the two ligaments that run alongside a joint to keep the joint from popping out to the side are called collateral ligaments because there are two of them, one on each side of the joint, that run parallel to each other. Similarly, in the stifle joint of the horse's hind limb, two ligaments cross each other and help provide front-to-back stability. Since their paths intersect and form a cross, they are called cruciate ligaments (from the Latin word for "cross").

Ligaments are constructed in a fashion much like tendons, with parallel, crimped fibers. (The largest ligament of the lower leg of the horse, the important suspensory ligament, also has some muscle tissue in it.) Ligaments, too, have important shock-absorbing functions.

Since the tissues are so similar, the same principles of injury and healing largely apply to both ligaments and tendons in the horse. However, treatments for various individual conditions of tendons and ligaments may be slightly different. In addition, the prognosis for recovery may differ slightly for various injuries. There's much more on those subjects later in this book. For now, look at where the major tendons and ligaments of the horse's lower limbs are located (see Figures 1 and 2).

THE MAJOR TENDONS AND LIGAMENTS OF THE LOWER FORELIMB

The Tendon of the Superficial Digital Flexor Muscle and Its Accessory Ligament

The superficial digital flexor muscle of the forelimb runs along the back of the big, long bone above the horse's knee, just below the skin (that bone is called the radius). As the muscle gets close to the horse's knee, it narrows and forms the superficial digital flexor tendon. In addition, part of the tendon is also formed by a strong, fan-shaped fibrous band that originates from just above the horse's knee, on the back inside part (posteromedial side, in anatomical terms) of the radius. This band is commonly known as the superior check ligament.

There are actually two check ligaments in the horse's forelimb (the other one will be talked about in connection with the deep flexor tendon). These ligaments get their name because it is believed that they "check" the stretching of the tendon. When weight is put on the horse's leg, as you know, the tendons and the ligaments on the back of the leg stretch. It's theorized that by having the firm attachment of a ligament holding the tendon to the bone, one that prevents or checks excessive stretching, the tendon is thereby partly protected from stretching beyond the limits of its strength.

The tendon thus formed goes through a canal on the back of the horse's knee, known as the carpal canal. In cross-section, the shape of the superficial flexor tendon is pretty round at this point, but as it continues down the horse's leg behind the cannon bone, the tendon flattens and becomes shaped like a half moon. Once the tendon gets

· Figure I ·

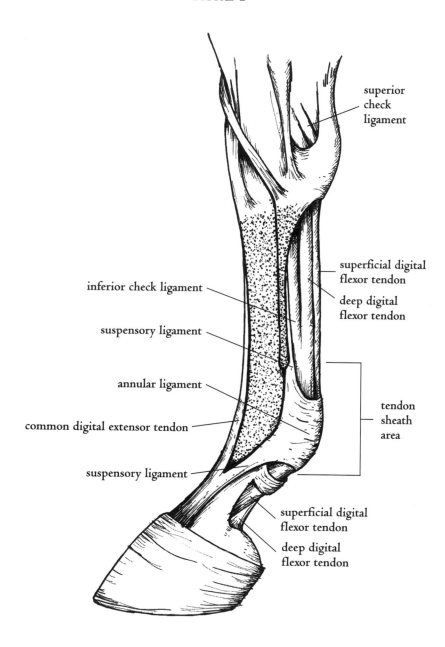

superior
check
ligament

superficial digital
flexor tendon

deep digital
flexor tendon

inferior check ligament

suspensory ligament

annular ligament

common digital extensor tendon

suspensory ligament

tendon
sheath
area

superficial digital
flexor tendon

deep digital
flexor tendon

The right foreleg, viewed from the medial (inside) side.

down to the level of the fetlock joint, it spreads out and gets a lot wider. As it goes down past the fetlock joint, the superficial flexor tendon separates into two branches and inserts into the bones of the pastern. The two branches of the tendon help support the bones of the pastern in this area.

The superficial flexor tendon is the most commonly injured tendon or ligament in the horse's leg. It's also the one that has been most extensively studied. Most of what's known about tendon and ligament injuries and healing in the horse has actually been determined on the superficial flexor tendon. The information gained from the study of this tendon has been applied to the other tendon and ligament structures in the horse's leg, under the assumption that the injury, healing and repair processes are the same in these other tissues as in the superficial flexor tendon.

The Tendon of the Deep Digital Flexor Muscle, Its Accessory Ligament and Tendon Sheath

In the horse's front leg, the deep digital flexor muscle actually is made up of three different parts. These join together at about the level of the knee to form the deep digital flexor tendon. Along with the superficial flexor tendon, the deep digital flexor tendon also passes through the carpal canal behind the knee. Its path runs just below (towards the bone) the superficial flexor tendon at this level (and throughout the limb). In cross-section the shape of the tendon changes from triangular to round as it descends the leg behind the cannon bone.

At about the middle of the cannon bone, the deep flexor tendon blends in with its accessory ligament, the inferior check ligament. As is the case with the superior check ligament of the superficial flexor tendon, it's thought that the inferior check ligament helps to keep the deep flexor tendon from stretching too far. The inferior check ligament starts up at

· FIGURE 2 ·

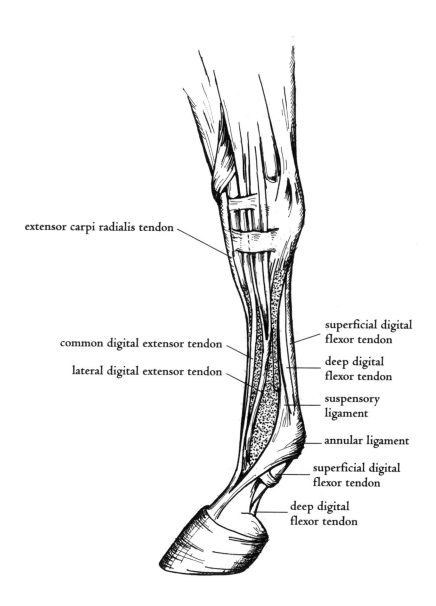

extensor carpi radialis tendon

superficial digital flexor tendon

common digital extensor tendon

deep digital flexor tendon

lateral digital extensor tendon

suspensory ligament

annular ligament

superficial digital flexor tendon

deep digital flexor tendon

The left foreleg, viewed from the lateral (outside) side.

the base of the horse's knee (carpus) and descends the leg until it joins the deep flexor tendon and becomes part of a single structure.

As the deep flexor tendon passes behind the fetlock, it goes through the tendon sheath. The tendon sheath is a channel through which the deep flexor tendon glides freely over the back of the fetlock joint as the horse moves and the leg bends. Normally the tendon sheath has fluid in it. This fluid helps to lubricate the movement of the tendon (among other functions, such as supplying nutrition to the tendon). In this regard, tendon sheath fluid is just like the fluid found in joints. The tendon sheath starts about two to three inches above the fetlock joint and extends about halfway down the horse's pastern.

At the level of the pastern, the deep flexor tendon shoots out from between the two sides of the divided superficial flexor tendon. Here, the tendon lies just below the skin. It can be easily identified if you feel around behind the horse's pastern. As it continues down the leg, the tendon widens and flattens. Once it gets into the foot, under the hoof, the tendon molds to the oblong contour of the navicular bone and passes right over the top of it. Finally, the deep flexor tendon ends by inserting into the bottom part of the horse's coffin bone (third phalanx).

Between the navicular bone and the deep flexor tendon is the navicular bursa. A bursa is a fluid-filled sac that lies between many tendons and bones in places where the tendon bends around the bone. (A bursa is like a pillow that cushions the tendon where it makes its bend). The navicular bursa is an important structure to consider when evaluating a horse with navicular disease (the subject of a later book).

For whatever reason, the deep flexor tendon is not commonly injured in horses. When injuries do occur, they most frequently are seen within the tendon sheath. The tendon sheath can become inflamed, too. Inflammation of the tendon sheath is called tenosynovitis. Tenosynovitis can occur with or without deep flexor tendon injury (see Figures 1 and 2).

The Suspensory Ligament

The horse's suspensory ligament is a broad strap of tissue that helps support the back of the horse's limb. It helps keep the fetlock joint from bending too far down when the horse bears weight on his leg. The suspensory ligament is frequently injured in all sorts of performance horses.

In the forelimb, the suspensory ligament originates from the base of the horse's knee. It descends down the back of the leg in a channel formed by the two splint bones (second and fourth metacarpal bones), right behind the horse's cannon bone and below the tendons (on the back side of the horse's cannon bone). As the ligament goes down the leg, it gradually gets farther away from the bone. At or just slightly below mid-cannon bone level, the suspensory ligament divides into two branches. These areas can be easily felt in the standing horse.

Each branch of the suspensory ligament attaches to the underlying sesamoid bone. (Two sesamoid bones occur at the back of the horse's fetlock joint. These little bones are thought to help support the ligament and distribute the stress on it as it bends around the joint.) Each branch crosses over its own sesamoid bone, goes around to the front of the pastern and ties into the large extensor tendon in the front of the leg. (See Figures 1 and 2.)

The Sesamoidean Ligaments

There are six major sesamoidean ligaments in the horse's limb. These little ligaments all attach to the sesamoid bones behind the horse's fetlock joint. They help to keep the fetlock joint from falling apart when the joint bends and they help keep all the bones in a fairly constant relationship to each other (see Figure 3). Given the fact that injuries to these ligaments heal slowly and poorly, fortunately injuries to the sesamoidean ligaments are rare. The sesamoidean ligaments are:

1. The intersesamoidean ligaments. These occur between the sesamoid bones. They help keep the sesamoid bones from spreading apart.

2. The collateral sesamoidean ligaments. These hold the sesamoid bones in place and are located on the inside and outside of the fetlock joint.

3. The straight sesamoidean ligament. The largest of the sesamoidean ligaments, it's a strap that runs down the back of the pastern, below the deep digital flexor tendon.

4. The oblique sesamoidean ligaments. These run from the base of the sesamoid bones, below and on either side of the straight sesamoidean ligament.

5. The cruciate sesamoidean ligaments. These small ligaments attach to the bottom of the sesamoid bones and provide further support to the base of the bones. They cross each other (hence the name "cruciate") and tie into the upper part of the pastern.

6. The short sesamoidean ligaments. These tiny ligaments are hard to see (and impossible to diagram). They lie just under the oblique sesamoidean ligaments.

The Annular (Palmar) Ligament of the Fetlock

The annular ligament is a thick band of tissue that runs over the back of the horse's fetlock joint. It actually forms the back wall of the tendon sheath in the area. The annular ligament is also tied down to both of the sesamoid bones. The ligament helps convert the space between the sesamoid bones into an actual canal through which the tendons can travel.

· FIGURE 3 ·

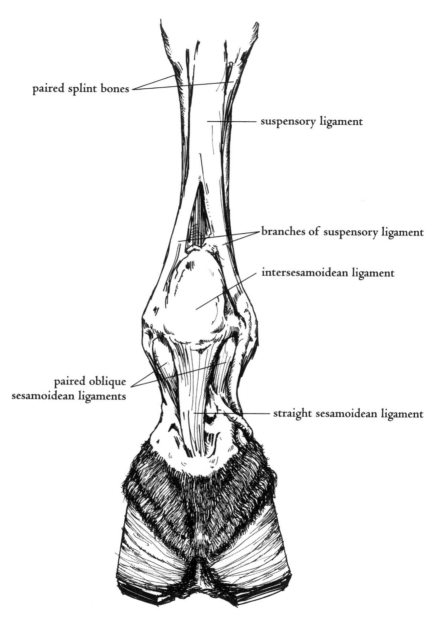

paired splint bones

suspensory ligament

branches of suspensory ligament

intersesamoidean ligament

paired oblique
sesamoidean ligaments

straight sesamoidean ligament

The major supporting structures of the back of the lower leg, viewed from behind the leg, with the overlying tendons and inferior check ligament removed.

The annular ligament has a very important stabilizing function for the tendons and the fetlock joint. It firmly binds the tendons to the back of the leg and thus helps direct their gliding movement. It's the wrapping paper that keeps the package that is the fetlock joint together (see Figures 1 and 2).

The annular ligament does become involved in a number of problems affecting tendons and ligaments. These problems are discussed in chapter 7, under Surgery.

The Extensor Tendons

Extension, stretching the horse's leg forward, is the opposite action of flexion. So it should come as no surprise that the extensor tendons are found on the opposite side of the leg from the flexor tendons. That is, the extensor tendons are on the front of the horse's leg. The extensor tendons function primarily to transmit the forces of the extensor muscles to the bones. They also help support the front side of the joints of the lower legs (see Figures 1 and 2).

Extensor tendons are rarely, if ever, hurt from overuse or strain. In fact, they are very rarely hurt at all. When they do get injured, usually it's from some sort of traumatic accident, such as a kick from another horse or a deep cut in the leg. Extensor tendon injuries are discussed in chapter 7.

There are three major extensor tendons in the horse's front leg:

1. The tendon of the extensor carpi radialis muscle. The large extensor carpi radialis muscle covers the front of the horse's forearm, right above the knee. Its large tendon goes over the top of the horse's knee joint and ties into the top of his cannon bone (the largest bone of the lower forelimb). When it passes over the knee, it travels through its own sheath, much like the tendon sheath of the deep digital flexor tendon (sometimes that sheath can get

swollen, too). The primary function of the extensor carpi radialis muscle and its tendon unit is to extend the horse's knee joint.

2. The tendon of the common digital extensor muscle. The common digital extensor muscle runs down the outside of the horse's forearm (next to the extensor carpi radialis muscle). Its tendon runs all the way down to the bone of the horse's foot (the coffin bone), where it attaches to a large prominence there. The common digital extensor tendon has its own tendon sheath where it runs over the knee, and its own bursa where it runs over the fetlock joint. The function of this tendon is to pull the lower leg and foot forward and to straighten the knee.

3. The tendon of the lateral digital extensor muscle. This is the smallest muscle-and-tendon unit of the front leg. The lateral digital extensor muscle lies behind the common digital extensor muscle. Its tendon runs down the leg beside the common digital extensor tendon and attaches to the top of the long pastern bone, just below the horse's fetlock joint. Like the common digital extensor tendon, the lateral digital extensor tendon has its own sheath where it runs over the knee, and its own bursa where it runs over the fetlock. This muscle-tendon unit also works to help extend the horse's foot and knee.

The Major Tendons and Ligaments of the Lower Hind Limb

Even though the tendons originate from different muscles, the anatomy of the structures of the horse's front and hind legs is quite similar below the level of the carpus (knee) or the tarsus (hock). In addition, the tendons and ligaments perform identical functions in the lower limbs of both the front and back legs (see Figure 4). However, there are some major differences in anatomy between the front and back legs:

· FIGURE 4 ·

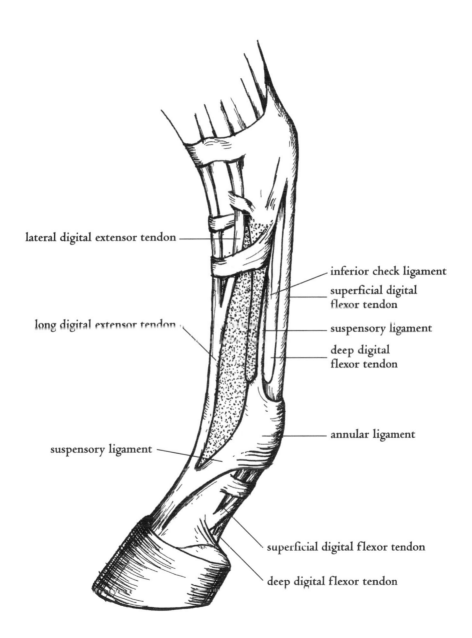

lateral digital extensor tendon

inferior check ligament

superficial digital
flexor tendon

long digital extensor tendon

suspensory ligament

deep digital
flexor tendon

annular ligament

suspensory ligament

superficial digital flexor tendon

deep digital flexor tendon

The left hind leg, viewed from the lateral (outside) side.

- There is no superior check ligament of the superficial flexor tendon in the hind limb.
- The inferior check ligament is thinner in the hind limb than in the front leg.
- The suspensory ligament is thinner, rounder and longer in the hind limb than in the forelimb.
- There are only two major extensor tendons of the hind limb (the long and lateral digital extensor tendons).

The tendons and ligaments of the hind limb are injured much less frequently than are the corresponding ligaments in the front leg. This is most likely because they are subjected to so much less stress. The horse normally bears about 70 percent of his weight on the front legs. As a result of this additional weight and stress, it's perhaps inevitable that the front legs get hurt more than the back legs. The principles of treatment of tendon and ligament injuries are identical for both front and hind limbs.

CHAPTER 2

How and Why Injuries Occur

TENDON AND LIGAMENT INJURIES ARE AMONG THE MOST frequently seen injuries of the musculoskeletal system of the horse. There is really no mystery as to how horses hurt their tendons and ligaments. They are injured as a result of stress and/or trauma. Stress that results in an injury to a tendon or ligament occurs in one of two ways.

Stress can be sudden and severe. With this type of injury, the stress on the horse's musculoskeletal system is so great that it overwhelms the ability of the tissue to tolerate it. The horse's leg just gives way, in the same manner that a stick would snap if you applied enough force to it. In this type of injury, the stress may be applied to the horse's leg in such a large and abnormal fashion that it exceeds the inherent strength of the tendons or ligaments in the leg. The tendon or ligament goes from being normal at one instant to being torn apart at the next. Such stress might be seen after a horse steps into a hole, for example.

An even more severe and obvious example of this type of stress would be some sort of penetrating wound. In some horses, the tendons may actually be partially or completely severed due to direct trauma to the leg.

17

(These cases aren't easy to overlook.) If the leg is cut or bleeding, you're not going to miss recognizing that there's a problem. This type of injury is quite different from simple inflammation of a tendon or a ligament and often requires aggressive medical and/or surgical intervention to try to save the horse.

Fortunately, dramatic, devastating injuries to the tendons and ligaments of the horse are not particularly common, at least in pleasure and most performance horses. The more common type of stress injury to horses appears to occur (according to current thinking) gradually and over time. This type of injury appears to be the result of an accumulation of small stresses to the tissue.

When a horse is working at peak performance levels, there's actually a very small margin of safety for his tendons and ligaments. It's been shown that the horse that's working hard is always right on the edge of exceeding the ability of these tissues to withstand the pressures placed on them. Certainly, if that ability to withstand stress is exceeded suddenly, the whole structure could conceivably give way and result in the type of devastating injury just mentioned.

More likely, though, given the inherent strength of tendons and ligaments, the whole structure won't give way all at once. Instead, small injuries to individual tendon or ligament fibers may occur over time. The injuries may be so small as to be undetectable. In this fashion, tendons or ligaments may be mildly and continuously injured. This results in an increasing cycle of inflammation, swelling and weakening of the affected structure. These little injuries may not be recognized until, finally, there is not enough normal tissue to withstand the strain of normal body movement. At that point, a large number of fibers may give way and a gross injury to the tendon can be seen to have occurred.

This type of stress is similar to that which happens when you bend and break a paper clip. You can bend a paper clip back and forth for a while with no apparent harmful effects to the clip. Suddenly, it weakens and snaps. The repeated bending has caused the metal in the paper clip to fatigue and ultimately give way. You can't really recognize the bits of individual strain that are occurring in the paper clip as you bend it back and forth. When it snaps, you know it immediately.

When a tendon or a ligament fatigues from repeated small injuries, the first things to go are the cross-links between the fibers. Next, some of the little fibers that make up the big cable that is the tendon or ligament give way. Tearing of fibers can occur anywhere in the tendon or ligament. Tears can occur on the edges or in the center of the affected tendon or ligament, or within the tendon sheath. (The specific location of a tear in a tendon or ligament is best seen with an ultrasound machine.)

You'll hear the term "core lesion" a lot when discussing tendon or ligament injuries. When a tear occurs in the center of the tendon or ligament, the tear is called a core lesion (a lesion is a general term that can be used to describe any sort of problem in any type of tissue). In a core lesion, the fibers that give way are in the middle, or core, of the tendon or ligament. Think of the injured tendon or ligament like a jelly doughnut. The doughnut is the tendon or ligament; the jelly in the middle is the tear. (If it's strawberry jelly, the jelly can even be thought of as the hemorrhage in the tendon or ligament.)

Factors Associated with Tendon and Ligament Injuries

Natural Stresses

Any time that the horse exercises, some sort of mechanical force gets applied to his legs. This stress is distributed to the legs in a predictable and measurable fashion. These "natural" stresses may make injury to certain parts of the leg inevitable. Repeated natural stresses to tissue can, if they become excessive, cause injury. Natural and unavoidable stresses on the horse's legs include:

- It has been shown that when horses canter, the superficial flexor tendon bears most of the early load. Perhaps this is one of the reasons why horses that canter a lot, like racehorses or event horses, have such a high incidence of injury to this structure.

- When horses perform at the extended trot, the suspensory ligament receives the early load when the leg is first put on the ground. This could be one of the reasons why there's a high incidence of suspensory ligament injuries in Standardbred racehorses. Jumping and dressage horses also seem to have a high incidence of suspensory ligament injuries.

- At any gait, it's been demonstrated that the fibers in the center of the superficial flexor tendon receive higher levels of stress than the fibers that are more on the edges of the tendon. Maybe that's why the central fibers are usually the first ones that rupture when the tendon is injured.

The Diameter of the Superficial Flexor Tendon

The superficial flexor tendon appears to be the most commonly injured tendon or ligament in the horse's leg. It's certainly the structure that's received the most study. In the tendon itself, the most commonly injured area lies roughly halfway between the knee joint and the fetlock joint. At this point, the diameter of the tendon is at its narrowest. It's thought by some veterinarians that this area may be something of an inherent weak point in the tendon.

Experimentally, when studies are done to test the strength of tendons (the tendon is literally pulled apart in a leg that has been removed from a dead horse), the middle of the tendon is the place where it always snaps.

It seems that this narrowed area is the part of the superficial flexor tendon that is least able to withstand stress. There is less tendon tissue at this point than anywhere else in the leg. It may therefore be in some ways inevitable that an injured superficial flexor tendon would give way at this point.

Crimp Problems

The center fibers of a tendon have less crimp in them than do the fibers on the outer edges. It may be that the center fibers are therefore less elastic than the fibers on the edges of the tendon. With less crimp, these fibers may have less ability to stretch and give than do other areas of the tendon. If the central fibers are less elastic, that could be one reason why they seem to be more frequently injured than other parts of the horse's tendons. Increasing age of the horse also decreases the amount of crimp of the tendon fibers.

Tendon Blood Supply

The blood supply to tendons may have something to do with where they get injured, according to some veterinarians. The mid–cannon bone level of the superficial flexor tendon and the fetlock area of the deep flexor tendon are areas where there is a decrease in the number of blood vessels (a "poor" blood supply, as it gets called) relative to the other areas of the tendon. Some veterinarians feel that this "poor" blood supply may make these areas more susceptible to injuries. In fact, injuries to the superficial and deep flexor tendons do occur most commonly in the areas where there are decreased numbers of blood vessels. Whether the blood supply has anything to do with it or not has not been confirmed, however.

Heat

Heat build-up in a tendon or ligament may have something to do with causing injury. When a horse exercises, his body tissues normally heat up a little bit. It's been demonstrated that the temperature in the center of the superficial flexor tendon (the "core" temperature) also goes up with exercise. Some veterinarians theorize that the increase in core tendon temperature may kill tendon or ligament cells over time. Alternatively, they think that possibly the increased tissue heat does something to mess up the normal metabolism of the cells and cause them to die. Either way, the build-up of heat may cause tendon or ligament cells to die and weaken the overall strength of the structure. It's another interesting theory that has yet to be proven.

Footing

Poor, uneven footing may have something to do with the occurrence of tendon and ligament injuries. If a horse lands unevenly or awkwardly, abnormal stresses may occur on the limb. The abnormal stress may cause an acute overload on the tendon or ligament.

Deep footing may also cause excessive tendon and ligament strain. It is theorized that if a horse is working on ground that is too soft or deep, his leg will sink deeply into the soft ground. It may sink so deeply that the tissue gets overstretched. As a result, it may tear. Alternatively, additional muscular effort may also be required to pull the horse's leg up out of deep ground. Over time, this extra work may ultimately contribute to fatigue and overuse of the tendons and ligaments.

Poor or Inadequate Conditioning

Inadequate conditioning and/or fatigue may play a role in the occurrence of tendon and ligament injuries. As previously mentioned, tendons and ligaments act like shock absorbers for the horse's leg. They stretch and they spring back with each step the horse takes.

However, muscles also have an important role in the absorption of shock. If muscles become tired due to exhaustion or inadequate training, they may not be able to perform in their normal elastic fashion. As the muscles tire, they then become stiff and less springy. This may result in extra stress being passed on to the tendons and ligaments. Ultimately, this extra stress may overload the system and cause something to break down.

Muscles strengthen with training. Therefore, if your horse is intended to be an athlete, proper conditioning is critical. In addition to building endurance in the horse's heart and lungs, proper training helps build the strength, coordination and flexibility that can help prevent tendon and ligament injuries.

Conditioning may not help tendons and ligaments, however. At this point in time it appears that conditioning does not help strengthen tendons and ligaments. In fact, too much training may just cause stress to these tissues and make them more prone to failure. It may also be true that we just don't know enough about tendons and ligaments to condition them.

Conformation

Some people try to blame a particular horse's conformation for tendon and ligament injuries. For example, it is theorized by some veterinarians that long toes or long, sloping pasterns contribute to tendon and ligament injuries. Here's why:

Long toes or sloping pasterns are supposed to make it harder for the horse to break over his hoof. When the horse moves forward, his foot hits the ground, usually heel first, and then breaks over the toe prior to the leg getting pulled back up into the air. When the horse's foot lands on the ground, the weight of the horse passing over the leg tends to drive the fetlock joint down into the ground. This causes the tendons and ligaments that run down the back of the lower limbs to stretch.

The conformation theory of tendon injuries is that the longer the toe or the longer and more sloping the pastern, the deeper the fetlock can be driven into the ground. If the fetlock were to be driven deep into the ground, it would then be theoretically harder for the horse to break over his toe, or at least it would take longer for him to do so. Thus, the tendons or ligaments in this situation might be forced to stretch even further or stay stretched for a longer time than "normal." More stress than normal could be applied to them under these circumstances.

Although this theory of conformation and tendon stress sounds like it should make a lot of sense, in fact there is no research to support it. Indeed, some observations that have been made on the effect of hoof angle and tendon stress would tend to contradict this theory (see chapter 10). Actually, no one can predict whether or not a horse will have tendon and ligament problems based solely on the conformation of his legs.

Boots and Bandages

Misapplied boots or bandages can surely cause injuries to the tendons and ligaments. Bandages or boots can be placed (improperly) in such a way as to cause constriction of the lower limb. Boots and bandages can act like rubber bands around the leg if they are put on too tightly. This can result in the so-called "bandage bow," a swollen leg caused by a bandage. Bandages and boots are not necessarily benign, nor are they necessarily even effective at doing what they purport to do. (There's more information about bandages and boots in chapter 9.)

Even though no one knows for sure how and why tendon and ligament injuries occur in the horse, still, the information gained from theorizing about how they occur may eventually help to prevent these injuries. Once they do occur, it's important to recognize them. That's the subject of the next chapter.

CHAPTER 3

Diagnosing an Injury

Some tendon and ligament injuries are obvious. A horse that has cut through the back of his front leg and severed the tendons has an injury that is pretty difficult to overlook. Such injuries are usually veterinary emergencies and often require surgery to correct. Severe injuries with disruption of the tendons and the suspensory ligament may even call for euthanasia of the unfortunate horse.

The tendon and ligament injuries that are of concern to most horse owners (and, happily, much more common) are rarely life-threatening. In their own way, however, they can be very serious. Many horses that sustain injuries to the tendons and ligaments cannot return to their previous level of performance, especially if the horse is expected to be a racehorse. Early recognition of these milder injuries, when possible, is important so that more severe damage can be prevented.

When tendons and ligaments are injured, they become inflamed. Inflammation of a tendon is called tendinitis. Inflammation of a ligament is called desmitis.

Inflammation is an important and exhaustively studied process that occurs in the horse's body as a result of injury or infection to any tissue. Inflammation is a necessary step in the body's healing process. The signs of inflamed tissue are predictable and well described. They were first described by the Romans! The classic signs of inflammation that follow are the things that are important to look for in a tendon or ligament to determine if your horse is developing an injury to these structures.

Signs of Injury

Heat

As a result of the process of inflammation, blood vessels dilate. This dilation causes the tissue to feel warm to the touch. The dilation of the blood vessels means that there is effectively more blood in the area. The warmth of the inflamed tissue can even be measured, using a technique known as thermography.

From a practical standpoint, however, heat is not a particularly useful diagnostic sign in assessing tendon and ligament injuries. Thermography has demonstrated that the temperature of inflamed tissue only goes up about one degree Fahrenheit. You really have to wonder if you are sensitive enough to pick up a one-degree rise in the temperature of a leg with your fingers. In fact, one study noted an increase in the heat of injured tendons in only 17.6 percent of the cases. If the horse is moving around a lot, or if it's hot outside anyway and you and the horse are sweating, it's pretty unlikely that trying to detect heat in a tendon or ligament is going to be a very rewarding experience.

The other problem with heat as a diagnostic tool is that it's not very precise. Thermography has shown that in tendon injuries, the whole leg heats up, not just the injured area. So even if you can determine that there has been an increase in the temperature of your horse's tendon or ligament, the increased heat is not likely to give you much of an idea where the injury has occurred.

If you do think that you feel heat in an injured leg, don't ignore it. Just don't expect heat to be the sensitive, accurate diagnostic sign that most people seem to think it is.

Swelling

Swelling of an injured tendon or ligament, like heat, occurs because the blood vessels get involved in the process. Inflammation is again the culprit.

Blood vessels are tubes that are actually made up of layers of cells closely wrapped together. With inflammation, the normally tight connections between the cells become leaky. This allows for fluid, which would normally be contained within the blood vessels, to leak out into the tissue. The tissue surrounding the blood vessels has to expand to accommodate the fluid leaking out into it. Consequently, you see swelling in the horse's leg.

Swelling can also occur as a result of bleeding into the tissue. With severe tendon or ligament injuries, blood vessels in and around the tendon can be torn. This also causes an obvious swelling in the tissue. Active bleeding within the tendon or ligament is a serious problem because the increased fluid in the tissue can further stretch and tear the already injured area.

Swelling of a tendon gives rise to the horseman's term for an injured tendon: a bowed tendon. As a result of an injury to a tendon, especially to the superficial flexor tendon, swelling that distorts the back of the leg often occurs. This swelling gives the back of the leg the characteristic bowed-out appearance that gives the injury its common name.

According to one study, swelling is the most common sign that is seen with injuries to tendons and ligaments. However, minor injuries may not swell very much at all. In addition, the covering that surrounds all of the tendons and ligaments in the upper leg is very thick and prevents most swelling from becoming apparent. Thus, it may not be possible to find swelling when an injury occurs high up in the suspensory ligament, for example, even if the injury is relatively severe.

Pain

When a tendon or ligament is injured, the area of the injury that is swollen and/or hot may also be painful. (This is at least partly due to the release of chemicals related to the inflammatory process.) If you squeeze the part of an injured tendon or ligament that seems swollen, the horse may let you know it hurts. He may try to jerk his leg away from you or run backwards or perform some other subtle reaction. (Squeezing a sore tendon is not something that you want to keep doing to your horse unless you like getting stepped on.)

Importantly, you have to hold the leg up in the air to see if the tendon or ligament that you suspect is injured really hurts. If you squeeze a tendon or ligament while the leg is on the ground, most horses won't react very dramatically, even if they have an injury. (Why this is true is anyone's guess.) In fact, not all injured tendons will be sensitive to the touch. In one study of 400 tendon injuries, only 20 percent of the horses showed a painful response to squeezing the injured area.

Trying to determine if a tendon or ligament really is painful to the horse does take some experience. Most horses normally don't enjoy having their tendons or ligaments squeezed. In the author's experience, this is especially true when you squeeze in and around the suspensory ligament. Horses generally hate having their suspensory ligaments squeezed. They may react to any sort of pressure over that area. Consequently, you have to be careful not to overreact to a horse pulling his leg away from you when you squeeze his tendons or ligaments. Just because he pulls his leg away from you when you pinch his tendon or ligament doesn't necessarily mean there's trouble there. It can also be helpful to try the same test on the other leg, to see if the horse reacts in the same manner. If he does, you either have two problems, or more likely, none at all.

Loss of Function (Lameness)

Many horses that have an injury to a tendon or a ligament feel enough pain to make them show lameness. That is, if a horse's leg hurts, he may not put as much weight on it as he otherwise would. Thus, he may very well limp on his injured leg. The accurate detection of lameness is something that requires time, experience and training, and is probably best left to your veterinarian.

Interestingly, not all horses that have sustained injuries to their tendons or ligaments will limp, particularly if the injury is relatively minor. The previously quoted study of 400 horses with tendon injuries identified only 40 percent of the horses as being lame. This can eventually result in some problems for the horse. If the horse doesn't show lameness and the owner hasn't noticed that the leg is swelling up (or maybe it's not swelling up at all), it is possible for a relatively minor injury to go on unchecked until it becomes a relatively major one.

Lack of lameness can be a particular problem in injuries involving the inferior check ligament or the suspensory ligament. For some reason, many horses with these injuries won't show lameness even with relatively severe damage to these structures.

An even more frustrating problem to diagnose can be horses that only limp occasionally. Injuries to the suspensory ligament are often like that. For example, horses with injuries to a branch of the lower suspensory ligament or high up at the origin of the suspensory ligament may show a lameness that is inconsistent. Lameness may be there one day and gone another. Lameness may be seen only in soft dirt (as opposed to a hard surface, which usually makes lameness worse) or it may be seen in the leg that is on the outside of a circle when the horse is trotted. Still, even if your horse's lameness doesn't seem "normal" or consistent, don't just ignore it and hope it will go away. Have it checked out by your veterinarian. You may be able to keep a relatively minor problem from turning into a bigger one.

Diagnosing Injuries

Flexion Tests

One of the commonly performed tests to determine lameness in the horse is the so-called flexion test. In this test, the horse's leg is held in the air, usually for about sixty seconds. The fetlock and the knee joints are bent fairly firmly (there's something of an art to this exam and it's impossible to describe how hard to flex the limb) and the horse is trotted off to see if he's lame or if his lameness increases.

Flexion tests are commonly thought to be tests for joint lameness. Indeed, sore joints don't like to be flexed. However, flexion tests are not very specific or precise for a source of limb lameness. When the leg is held up in the air and the joints are flexed, actually all of the tissues of the lower leg are somehow affected. For example, the flexor tendons and the major ligaments get all crunched together during a flexion test. If these tissues are sore, performing a flexion test on the limb also may worsen lameness related to them. Don't get fooled into thinking that your horse's positive response to a flexion test means that he has a joint problem and that the tendons and ligaments are all right.

Digital Pressure Tests

The fact that an injury to a tendon or ligament may hurt when it is squeezed can be very useful diagnostically. Digital pressure tests are performed in much the same fashion as are flexion tests. If a swollen or sore part of a horse's tendon or ligament is suspected as a problem, trotting the horse after applying pressure to the area can be helpful in deciding if the swelling really means trouble or not. If, immediately after putting pressure on a tendon or ligament injury, the horse is observed to be lame, or the existing lameness increases, that swelling may well be significant.

A swelling in a tendon or ligament that isn't painful, or that isn't associated with increased lameness after pressure, is more likely to be insignificant, although it may reflect a previous injury to the area. Swellings around tendons or ligaments can also be a result of some other problem (such as an infection in the leg or some sort of local trauma).

Local Anesthetic "Blocks"

Although they are less commonly used in the diagnosis of tendon and ligament injuries than in the diagnosis of other causes of lameness in the horse, the use of local anesthetics to help pinpoint the area of soreness in a horse's leg can sometimes be quite helpful. Local anesthetic blocks are especially helpful in diagnosing lameness that originates from the upper suspensory ligament areas (known as proximal suspensory desmitis).

When a horse's leg hurts from an injury, he limps. If, by using a local anesthetic, you can make the area that hurts numb, the horse won't limp anymore. Once the horse stops limping, you can deduce where the problem is. You can then perform a more detailed examination of the injured area and begin treatment.

Ultrasound

In the early 1980s, veterinarians began to use diagnostic ultrasound to examine the tendons and ligaments of the lower limb of the horse (diagnostic ultrasound is different from therapeutic ultrasound; therapeutic ultrasound is discussed in chapter 11). The procedure has been truly revolutionary in advancing the understanding of tendon injuries. The technology is quite common and used for many different purposes. For example, boats send sound waves down into the water to detect sub-marines under the surface (it's called sonar). Ultrasound technology permits mothers to see their developing babies.

In ultrasound, a high-frequency sound wave is sent into tissue by a probe. The tissue reflects the sound wave. The reflected sound wave is picked up and analyzed by the same ultrasound probe that sent out the wave. A computer then analyzes reflected sound waves and generates an image of the tendons and ligaments. This image can then be seen on the screen of the ultrasound machine. The image on the ultrasound screen is made up of blacks, whites and grays and looks rather complicated. Actually, since there are not very many structures in the horse's lower leg, it's not terribly hard to distinguish the structures, once you have the training.

An injury to a tendon or a ligament cannot be accurately diagnosed without the use of ultrasound. In fact, it has been estimated that if you use your hands and eyes alone in trying to diagnose tendon and ligament injuries, you will make a mistake 75 percent of the time! Needless to say, if you really want to find out what's going on in your horse's injured tendon or ligament, you have to do an ultrasound examination.

Ultrasound exams help determine the severity of an injury to a horse's limb. They can be very helpful in guiding treatment and following the progress of recovery. It is important to realize, however, that an injured tendon or ligament is not ready to go back to full work as soon as the ultrasound examination is normal. An ultrasound examination looks normal before the tissue is actually fully healed and ready to withstand normal work. Many veterinarians recommend that at least two months pass between the first normal ultrasound examination after the initial injury and the time that the horse is started back to full work.

· Figure 5 ·

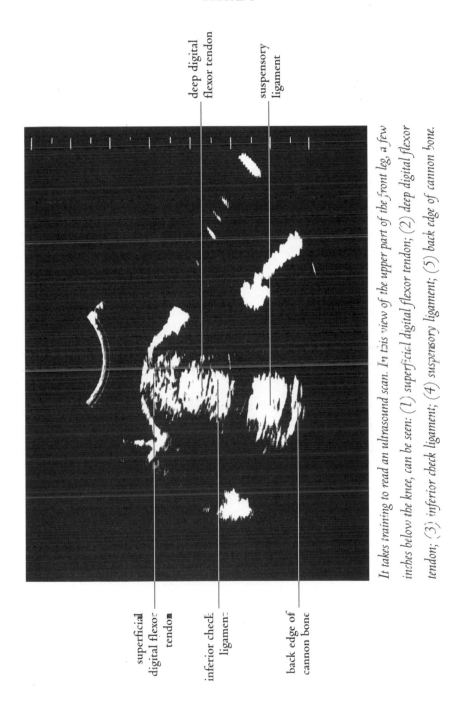

deep digital
flexor tendon

suspensory
ligament

superficial
digital flexor
tendon

inferior check
ligament

back edge of
cannon bone

It takes training to read an ultrasound scan. In this view of the upper part of the front leg, a few inches below the knee, can be seen: (1) superficial digital flexor tendon; (2) deep digital flexor tendon; (3) inferior check ligament; (4) suspensory ligament; (5) back edge of cannon bone.

If you don't have access to a veterinarian with an ultrasound machine, you have to proceed very cautiously in treating your horse's injury. You sort of have to assume the worst: that the tendon is badly injured and that it will take a lot of time to bring your horse back to his normal work. The alternative is to start him back to work too early and re-injure the horse. Some legs that appear quite swollen don't have injured tendons or ligaments; some relatively minor swellings conceal relatively major problems. An ultrasound machine can help your veterinarian tell the difference. Even if you don't have ready access to an ultrasound machine, if your horse hurts a tendon or ligament, it may well be worth your time to take your horse to someone who does.

Radiographs (X rays)

Radiographs are generally not very useful in the diagnosis of tendon and ligament injuries. Tissues that normally contain a lot of water, such as tendons and ligaments, often do not show up well on a radiograph. Very occasionally, in old tendon or ligament injuries, radiographs may demonstrate that parts of the tissue have calcified due to chronic inflammation. Most of the time X rays just don't help in making a diagnosis of a tendon or ligament injury.

However, it is possible for the bones to become involved when there are tendon and ligament problems, especially when the problems involve the suspensory ligament. Three major areas of bone fracture can be occasionally observed in association with suspensory ligament problems.

I. Bone at the origin of the suspensory ligament, at the back and base of the horse's knee, may sometimes pull loose from the cannon bone when this area is injured. When this happens, fragments of bone can be seen on X rays. These are called avulsion fractures. In an avulsion injury, instead of the ligament tearing, small pieces of bone are actually pulled away from the underlying bone.

34

2. The paired sesamoid bones, behind the horse's fetlock joint, can fracture due to weight-bearing stress. It is impossible for a sesamoid bone to fracture without having some inflammation in the overlying branch of the suspensory ligament and/or the sesamoidean ligaments.

   Of course, not all horses that have inflamed branches of their suspensory ligaments have sesamoid bone fractures. However, when sesamoid bone fractures occur, it complicates the prognosis for the horse's recovery. Frequently, some sort of surgery is recommended to treat horses with sesamoid bone fractures.

3. The paired splint bones (the second and fourth metacarpal or metatarsal bones in the front and back legs, respectively) may fracture due to weight-bearing stress. This can occur in association with suspensory ligament strain. In addition, when a fracture occurs, it causes some inflammation of the bone in the surrounding area. This causes new bone to be produced. This lump of new bone, called a callus, can put pressure on the suspensory ligament and cause secondary inflammation there (sort of like having a rock in your shoe). The treatment for this condition is surgical removal of the bump or the part of the fractured splint bone below the fracture site.

By using some or all of the proper diagnostic techniques, the extent of a tendon or ligament injury can be accurately assessed. Fortunately, the diagnosis of these problems is usually fairly straightforward. After you've figured out the problem, the next step in solving it is to begin proper medical treatment.

CHAPTER 4

How Injuries Heal

Tendons and ligaments don't heal with normal tendon and ligament tissue. This is something of a problem. If you cut your skin, for example, and it's sewn back together, the body is only too happy to resume normal skin function, leaving only a small scar. In horse tendons and ligaments, on the other hand, the horse's body can't do this. After they are injured, tendons and ligaments never return to their pre-injury "normal" state.

When a tendon or ligament is first injured, when the tissue is stretched beyond its ability to withstand stress, the tissue tears. Fibers that make up the structures separate and the local blood vessels tear and bleed.

Bleeding can have many negative effects on the injured tendon or ligament. The loss of blood supply to the injured tissue may result in further tissue death due to a lack of oxygen. The bleeding in the injured tissue also causes swelling. The accumulation of blood in the tendon may further serve to separate or damage tendon fibers that may not have been torn during the initial injury. Bleeding in a tendon or ligament may also result in a larger, more discrete collection of blood called a hematoma (a localized accumulation of blood in tissue). The initial injury also initiates the process of inflammation.

Inflammation is an important local protective response to the injury to the tendon or ligament, initiated by the horse's body. It's part of normal healing. Inflammation is an incredibly complex process, one that has been extensively studied. It's responsible for the classic signs of tissue injury that were described in the preceding chapter. It's a good thing. The process of inflammation helps break down and remove the damaged tissue in the horse's leg.

However, inflammation is also a process that is important to direct and control if the best healing of the horse's tendon or ligament injury is expected to occur. Inflammation that runs around unchecked is a bad thing. In fact, inflammation in an injured tendon or ligament can be a double-edged sword.

Inflammation causes the release of white blood cells (leukocytes) into the injured area of the tendon or ligament. These cells release enzymes (enzymes are proteins that help break down complex chemical structures to more simple components). These enzymes help dissolve damaged tissue and thereby help it to be removed via the circulatory system of the horse's body. Unfortunately, enzymes are not selective in their effects. They do not simply remove the damaged tissue and then stop. Thus, the process of inflammation, if it goes along unchecked, can further increase the damage to the injured tissue by causing chemical enzyme damage to the healthy tissue in the area.

After the process of inflammation has subsided, the injured fibers of the tendon or ligament are replaced. Adequate replacement of the injured fibers is really the biggest problem involved in the healing of tendon and ligament injuries. Injuries to these tissues do not and cannot heal with normal tendon and ligament tissue. They heal with scar.

Just like normal tendons and ligaments, scar tissue is made up largely of collagen. (Collagen is a protein that makes up much of the non-bone tissue of the horse's body.) The type of collagen in scar is quite different from that in normal tissue, however. Collagen in scar tissue has less tensile strength than does normal tendon or ligament tissue (it pulls apart more easily). The scar tissue that forms in the injured tissue is laid down in a random and haphazard pattern, not in the parallel, crimped fiber pattern of normal tissue. In addition, abnormal cross-linking of the scar tissue occurs.

With time and healing, the scar tissue that forms in the tendon does eventually mature. It becomes stronger and the fibers begin to orient themselves in a more parallel fashion. Part of the therapy for healing tendons is to encourage organization in this fashion. Mild, early exercise for horses recovering from tendon and ligament injuries is now considered very important for ideal tendon healing. Weight bearing during exercise helps the collagen fibers of the healing scar tissue to re-establish a parallel arrangement. If injured tendons or ligaments are continuously rested, bandaged and immobilized, this may result in a decrease in the ultimate strength of the healing tissue that can never be regained. Whatever the case, it is important to remember that no matter how much time for healing is given to an injured tendon or ligament, it never regains its full, pre-injury strength.

Adhesions are bits of scar tissue that cause the healing tendon or ligament to stick abnormally to other bits of surrounding tissue. Post-injury adhesions are a complication of tendon or ligament healing that is less than ideal. Adhesions form as a result of inflammation in the injured tissue; one goal of directing the healing process is to minimize their formation. A tendon or ligament that has healed with large amounts of adhesions cannot glide or operate in a normal fashion. Early return to mild exercise in the injured limb may also help prevent adhesion formation because it encourages the tissue to move. Unfortunately, some degree of adhesion formation may be inevitable in severe injuries.

If the healing that occurs after a tendon or ligament injury is ideal, there will be minimal adhesion formation and the repaired structure will be as strong as possible. If ideal healing does not occur, the normal strength, elasticity and movement of the injured structure may never be regained. Healing takes time, sometimes up to a year or more. You just have to be patient with your horse; he's healing as fast as he can. Horses don't (and can't) heal any faster than people do. Proper treatment of injured tendons and ligaments gives them their best chance to return to as normal a function as possible.

CHAPTER 5

Medical Treatment of Acute Injuries

If you look at the studies that have been done, one thing becomes clear: In spite of all the investigations that have been done on horse tendons and ligaments and all the advances that have been made in veterinary care for the horse, the incidence of tendon and ligament injuries and the effectiveness of treatment for them has not significantly changed much over the years. No method of treatment of these injuries has been devised that provides an effective cure for the problem. Furthermore, no one approach has been shown to give the "best" healing. In fact, the tendons and ligaments of the horse have not received the same study and attention as have other tissues, such as the bones, cartilage or joints. More study of these injuries is needed.

There are no miracles out there when it comes to trying to get a tendon or a ligament to heal. (Not that there aren't people out there who say they have some miracles to sell you.) Dealing with tendon and ligament injuries is frustrating. Mostly, healing takes a lot of time. Unfortunately, many impatient owners seem to be unable to accept this fact. They feel it is important to do something, whether it makes any medical sense or not. Further complicating matters is the fact that not all veterinarians agree on the "best" method for treating injured tendons and ligaments. In order to get the best healing possible for your horse, however, you should at least try to follow some established principles.

When you treat a horse for a tendon or ligament injury, you really have only two goals. First of all, you want to try to return the structure of the tendon to as close to its pre-injured state as possible. Secondly, you want to try to minimize the formation of scar tissue in and around the injured tissue. The presence of scar tissue in a tendon or ligament changes the way the tissue behaves. Scar tissue makes the structure less strong than it was before it was injured. It also reduces the ability of the injured tendon or ligament to stretch.

In order to control scar tissue formation, the initial treatment efforts are directed toward trying to keep the inflammatory response to the minimum amount necessary to repair the tendon or ligament. You also want to try to keep the inflammation from bothering the rest of the normal tendon or other structures in the area.

As mentioned before, inflammation is a natural process that occurs when a tendon or ligament gets injured. It is an important process that is required for the healing of any tissue. However, you also want to control the response so that the inflammation doesn't get excessive. Medical therapy for tendon and ligament inflammation is prescribed in recognition of what's going on in the tissue while the horse is healing. Within the first few hours after you've recognized that your horse has hurt a tendon or a ligament, your goal must be to try to control as much inflammation as possible. You are trying to control the bleeding, swelling and damage to the newly injured tissue. Several methods of therapy can be very useful in helping you to achieve this goal.

COLD THERAPY

Application of cold things to a limb with a tendon or ligament injury is a time-honored and very effective way to help stop the inflammatory process. Ice, chemical cold packs, or refrigerated and reusable ice bandages are all great ways to apply cold to a leg. A cold water hose may help, too. In reality, though, the colder you can get the leg, the better. Cold helps cause the blood vessels that have dilated in inflammation to constrict so that they won't leak fluid or blood. Cold also helps to slow down the release and activity of the harmful chemicals that are released during the inflammatory process, and it helps decrease the pain that the horse feels from his injury.

You can really help your horse's injury a lot by keeping it cold. It's pretty hard to apply cold therapy too frequently, although you don't want to do it for too long at one time. You can hurt tissue if you keep it too cold (that's what happens in skiers who get frostbite). Additionally, the blood vessels in tissue that gets too cold will dilate when the cold is removed; this reflex action could conceivably increase swelling and bleeding in an acutely injured tendon or ligament. If you can do several thirty- to sixty-minute sessions of cold therapy a day for the first several days, you will really be doing a lot toward getting your horse started down the road to ideal healing of his tendon or ligament problem.

BANDAGING

Bandaging the injured tendon or ligament is a good way to help control the swelling. The pressure of a bandage helps keep swelling to a minimum. Obviously, if there's a reasonable amount of pressure on the outside of the limb, the fluid that's trying to leak out as a result of bleeding and inflammation isn't going to be able to move out into the tissue as easily. Fluid accumulation in a tendon or ligament leads to the formation of scar tissue. As has been discussed, that's not something you want in the injured tissue.

A bandage should apply a firm, even pressure over the whole limb. It should be changed at least daily so that pressure points don't arise underneath the bandage. Bandage pressure can be applied in addition to cold therapy, using a refrigerated wrap, or you can apply ice over the top of a firmly applied bandage. Medicated bandages, such as a modified Unna's boot (commercially available as Gelocast) can also give some degree of support to an injured leg. (This type of bandage, which was actually developed in the late 1800s, is favored by some veterinarians although its actual benefits are a subject for discussion.) Whatever you use and whichever way you bandage a leg that has an injured tendon or ligament, just do it.

Rest

In the early stages of treatment for acute tendon injuries, complete stall rest is very important for the horse. Although horses are not at all cooperative patients and hardly rest in the true sense of the word, confinement in the stall is very important in the first few days following an acute tendon or ligament injury. Any exercise after an acute tendon or ligament injury, especially in the first forty-eight hours, has the potential to make the injury worse.

Nonsteroidal Anti-Inflammatory Drugs

Drugs to control pain and inflammation are always useful in the treatment of acute tendon and ligament injuries. Nonsteroidal anti-inflammatory drugs such as phenylbutazone (bute) or flunixin meglumine (Banamine) help interfere with the production of chemicals associated with the inflammatory process. This helps keep the inflammatory process under control. Since the drugs work along slightly different pathways, sometimes they are used in conjunction with each other to try to get a more potent effect. No one drug is necessarily better than another. Which particular anti-inflammatory drug is used for the treatment of tendon and ligament injuries is often a matter of the experience of the veterinarian treating the case.

It's probably best that horses recovering from tendon and ligament injuries do not receive nonsteroidal anti-inflammatory drugs for long periods of time. Although they are very effective at controlling swelling and inflammation in the injured tissue, they also have an undesirable side effect of suppressing the growth of the tissue that forms to repair the injury. There's no scientific data to evaluate the effect of long-term use of drugs like bute on healing tendons and ligaments, but it would seem reasonable to reduce their use to only that which is needed to control the acute swelling and inflammation.

Corticosteroids: Systemic and Intralesional

Corticosteroids are a group of very potent anti-inflammatory drugs. Many different corticosteroids are used for therapy of a variety of conditions of the horse. They are all very powerful drugs.

In the treatment of tendon and ligament injuries, some veterinarians inject corticosteroids into the horse's veins as a way to help reduce overall inflammation. Other veterinarians have injected corticosteroids into the injured areas. Local injections of corticosteroids into the injured site, however, have a very limited place in the treatment of tendon and ligament injuries in horses. This is because they have a number of undesirable side effects.

45

First, local corticosteroid injections can delay the healing of injured tendon and ligament tissue for up to a year. They also reduce the strength of the ultimate repair. Corticosteroid injections directly into the site of the injury have been shown to cause the injured tissue to calcify in some cases. (This would have the effect of making the injured tissue brittle and subject to re-injury. Calcium is a mineral and doesn't stretch like normal tissue.) There are other, safer methods of decreasing inflammation within a tendon or ligament than injections of corticosteroids.

Corticosteroids can occasionally be effective for the relief of inflammation around a tendon, such as occurs with inflammation of the tendon sheath. When tendon sheath inflammation is treated with corticosteroids, the corticosteroids are commonly combined with hyaluronic acid (HA). This combination of drugs helps to increase the anti-inflammatory effect. (The combination may also help improve the normal gliding of the tendon that occurs in the tendon sheath, since hyaluronic acid is a soft tissue lubricant.)

BAPN (Beta-Aminoproprionitrile)

Soon there may be a new treatment for tendon and ligament injuries in the horse. There's a lot of work currently being done on horses with tendinitis with a drug called beta-aminoproprionitrile, or BAPN.

As you know, when tendons and ligaments heal, the collagen initially formed to heal the injured area is somewhat haphazard and unorganized. Over time, the new tissue gets arranged in a more normal fashion with parallel fibers. Like normal tendons, these fibers in the newly formed tissue are also tied to each other from side to side by fibrous cross-links (imagine the fibers holding hands with each other). These cross-links give the newly formed tissue in the healing tendon or ligament stability and strength. Unfortunately, in healing tendons or ligaments, the cross-linking process may not occur in a fashion similar to normal, uninjured tendons.

BAPN helps to prevent this cross-linking process. At the tissue level, this has the effect of decreasing the formation of scar tissue. It may be that by helping stop the cross-linking, a more rapid formation of normal, parallel fibers is promoted. BAPN has been shown to be effective in reducing scar tissue formation in people with healing wounds. One study has shown it to be effective in making injured horse tendons look better more quickly (as evaluated by ultrasound) as well.

What is not yet known about BAPN is how well it works in the long term. That is, even though the tendon looks better in the short term, what is the end result of the healing process when the drug is used on an injured tendon or ligament? The scar that forms in the healing tendon or ligament is part of the normal healing process; if you reduce the scar, do you also reduce the ultimate strength of the healed tissue? Do you reduce the speed at which healing is achieved? What is the proper dose and best way to give the drug? These questions need to be answered and the drug is currently under investigation. It shows considerable promise and when the questions are answered satisfactorily, there may be a new treatment to look forward to for tendon and ligament injuries in horses.

Hyaluronic Acid (HA; Sodium Hyaluronate)

Hyaluronic acid is a substance occurring naturally in the horse's body. It has numerous functions in the body and is found in particularly high concentrations in joints, tendon sheaths and the eye.

Injections of HA next to tendon or ligament injuries have been used by some veterinarians in an effort to help promote healing. In people, HA injections have been useful for the treatment of injured tendons in the hands. Experimentally, it's been recognized that the hyaluronic acid concentration goes up around tendon tissue that has been recently injured. It's thought that HA helps keep the injured area hydrated and helps promote tissue repair. (However, the HA that's released by the injured tissue is rapidly broken down by inflammatory enzymes.) Adding HA to wounds, to replace what's been used up in the inflammatory process, has been shown to cause more rapid healing with less adhesion formation in some species.

HA injections have also been advocated for the treatment of problems that occur within the sheathed areas of the tendons. Within the tendon sheath, the tendon normally glides. Injuries in the sheathed area can result in adhesion formation. Adhesions cause the injured tendon to stick inside the sheath, resulting in pain and a decrease in normal function. HA injections into an injured tendon sheath may be of some use in helping to decrease the formation of these adhesions and in improving the normal gliding action.

Unfortunately, in the studies that have been done on horses, the clinical results of using HA in tendon and ligament injuries that occur in the unsheathed areas have been pretty disappointing. In one study, when tendon inflammation was caused by injecting a chemical into a tendon and the leg was treated with HA, there was no improvement in healing gained by injecting HA next to the healing tissue compared to what was seen in the untreated controls.

Furthermore, adhesion formation in the nonsheathed areas of tendons or ligaments may not be that big a deal. The importance of gliding in this part of the leg isn't known. Adhesions in these areas may even be of benefit if they serve as a source of additional blood supply to the healing tendon (this hasn't been demonstrated either, however).

Finally, some veterinarians have given favorable reports on the results of injecting HA directly into tendon lesions. In their hands, the results of injection into (instead of beside) the injured area is of benefit in decreasing inflammation and spreading healing. Direct injection into the tendon can be accompanied by intravenous administration of HA at the same time. This is done in the hopes that a more favorable environment for healing can be created for the injured area.

Polysulfated Glycosaminoglycan (PSGAG; Adequan)

The use of PSGAGs is becoming increasingly popular for the treatment of tendon and ligament injuries in horses, although their clinical effectiveness still hasn't been proven. Although primarily intended as a form of therapy for joints, PSGAGs may have some effect on healing tendons and ligaments. In fact, the microscopic structure of a tendon or ligament is remarkably similar to the cartilage that covers the surfaces of the joints in the horse's body. PSGAGs are potent anti-inflammatory compounds that help inhibit the destructive enzymes that are released into the injured tissue. In addition, PSGAGs may help stimulate the formation of collagen in the healing tissue.

For treatment of tendon and ligament injuries, PSGAG can be given in the muscle, according to the manufacturer's recommendations. Additionally, a preliminary study done in England suggested that injecting the stuff directly into tendon lesions caused healing to be accelerated and improved. Unfortunately, another English study suggested that horses treated with PSGAG for their tendon injuries had a higher rate of re-injury than did horses that were not given injections into the tendon. The jury is still out on this form of treatment, but it does show some promise.

DMSO

DMSO is a chemical solvent that is credited with a number of remarkable properties that are useful in the treatment of inflammation. The most important property seems to be the neutralization of some of the destructive chemical substances that are released during inflammation. It also has some effect in protecting tissue from the effects of ischemia (lack of blood supply; you can make your finger ischemic by putting a rubber band around it).

In the treatment of tendon and ligament injuries, DMSO has been used in a number of ways. It can be given in a dilute intravenous solution, or orally via a nasogastric tube. Administered this way, it is hoped that DSMO will go through the horse's system and exert its anti-inflammatory effects where needed. Unfortunately, most of the damage will have been done and the inflammatory chemicals will have already been released by the time you can get DMSO into the horse. Still, it might do some good and it surely can't hurt. The stuff is really pretty harmless. It's easy to tell when a horse has been treated with it, however: If you give a horse DMSO in the vein or via a nasogastric tube, you'll be able to smell him in the barn for a couple of days.

DMSO liquid or gel is also commonly applied to the skin of horses that have sustained tendon or ligament injuries. It can be applied directly or under a bandage. DMSO can go through the skin without disrupting it. It's hoped that by using it on the skin, there will be local anti-inflammatory effects in the underlying tissue. Be careful, though. DMSO can be mildly irritating to the skin of some horses and cause burns or blisters.

In addition to its own benefits, DMSO can be used as a carrier for other substances. When DMSO is mixed with corticosteroids, for example, the level of corticosteroids in the tissue is increased by a factor of three! This could conceivably increase the beneficial anti-inflammatory effects over what could be obtained from DMSO alone. In combination with other drugs, DMSO is also frequently applied in the so-called sweat wrap (see chapter 6 for more information on sweat wraps).

Some veterinarians feel that DMSO should only be used for the first few days of treatment of a tendon or ligament injury, or until the fluid is removed from the injured tissue. This usually takes about a week. There's some evidence to suggest that DMSO has a harmful effect on the amount and quality of the collagen that forms in the scar tissue healing the injury. Therefore, some veterinarians say that DMSO therapy should be stopped after the first week.

DMSO is very volatile. Some people report that they can taste it when it gets on their skin. That's because DMSO is absorbed rapidly through the skin and gets into the circulation. When it reaches the lungs, it leaves the blood system and gets exhaled across the taste buds on the tongue. This certainly isn't harmful, but it's not the sort of thing you want to do before going out to eat at a nice restaurant.

Curiously, as much as DMSO is used, there are no standard dosage or treatment regimens you can follow for it. No controlled studies have been done to see how well the stuff really works in treating tendon and ligament injuries. The use of DMSO in treating tendon and ligament injuries is generally based on the experience of the veterinarian.

At this point in time, there is clearly no "best" way to treat an acutely injured tendon or ligament. How the tissue reacts to injury and heals is under investigation. It's likely that, as time goes by and as information is gathered, a combination of some or all of the above treatments will be appropriate for your horse. Medicine is an evolving process and the evolution of treatment for tendon and ligament injuries is in its infancy.

Once the acute phase of inflammation has been controlled, additional therapy and rehabilitation begin. It will be a long road back to recovery for your horse with most tendon and ligament injuries. The next chapter will give you information on how to make sure you're going in the right direction.

CHAPTER 6

The Healing Process: Therapy, Rehabilitation and Return to Work

In the first few days after injury to a tendon or ligament, your therapy is directed toward controlling the inflammatory response, as you read in chapter 5. After inflammation is controlled, the next important steps in rehabilitating a healing tendon or ligament are directed toward guiding the repair process. You would like to encourage the horse's body to produce the strongest and most functional tissue possible, as quickly as possible (if for no other reason than so you can start riding again!). Some tendon or ligament injuries may even be best treated by some sort of surgery (see chapter 7 for a discussion of surgical treatments).

When it comes to treating tendon and ligament injuries, you really have only two choices for therapy: You can let nature take its course, or you can take steps to direct the repair process.

"NATURAL" HEALING

Rest/Turning the Horse Out to Pasture

Prior to the advances in the understanding of tendon and ligament injuries that have been made in the past twenty or so years, the universal therapy for the treatment of these problems was to turn the horse out in a big pasture. After the initial injury was recognized, the horse might be confined for a short period of time, but then he would ultimately be let out into a big space where he could "heal" on his own. The horse would generally run around for a year or so, then be "ready" to go back to work.

From a time, expense and labor-saving standpoint, this is certainly the easy way to go. In fact, some horses will have significant healing in an injured tendon or ligament if they are left alone in a pasture for long enough. Time does heal many wounds. Taking care of an injured tendon or ligament by turning the horse out is certainly the least labor-intensive form of treatment. By ignoring the problem, you are hoping that it will just go away. (Unlike many of life's problems, sometimes it does!)

The problem with extended turnouts of horses with tendon and ligament injuries is that you can't really be sure what is going to happen to them. Some horses that are turned out to pasture for their injuries don't heal at all. A horse in pasture may continue to run around on his injured leg. Instead of healing, the injured tissue gets subjected to repeated stress and trauma. After all, horses are rotten medical patients and they refuse to take care of themselves. It's not as if they are going to rest and allow the tissue to heal. The author has seen horses return from extended turnouts of up to eighteen months with injuries that look little improved (or worse) than they did prior to being turned out.

The point is that unsupervised rehabilitation of a horse with a tendon or ligament injury is a bit of a double-edged sword. When horses heal in pasture, they do it well and with a minimum of time, effort and bother to their owners. When they don't heal, the owner may end up with a mess on his hands. Instead of having a horse that's ready to go back to work, the owner may have effectively wasted all the time the horse was given to heal. Furthermore, the repaired tissue may not be as strong as that which has been healing under the influence of controlled exercise. A tendon that has repaired itself strongly enough to withstand pasture exercise may not be strong enough to withstand the stress of jumping or racing.

Pasture turnout is probably not worth the risk in valuable horses, where optimum recovery and tissue repair is desired. To get the best recovery from your horse's tendon or ligament injury, you really should monitor him carefully.

Directing the Repair Process

Removal of Fluid

As the inflammatory process is being controlled or arrested, you need to take some steps to try to get the fluid that accumulates as a result of the injury out of the injured tendon or ligament. Tissue fluid and inflammatory proteins in the injured tissue provide a framework for the formation of scar tissue. It's important to try to get as much fluid out of the leg as possible and to do it as quickly as possible, before significant amounts of scar tissue form. Scar tissue formation begins four to six days after the injury has occurred. There are several ways to try to get fluid out of an injured tendon or ligament, including surgery (discussed in chapter 7).

Heat

Heat causes blood vessels to dilate. Once the inflammatory process has subsided, dilating the blood vessels in the limb may be one way to help get fluid out of it. Some veterinarians choose to use alternating cycles of hot and cold therapy to try to stop inflammation and encourage fluid removal at the same time (no one has ever studied how well this actually works). There are a couple of things that are commonly done to horses in an effort to encourage heat in tissue.

Sweat Wraps Sweat wraps are bandages that are applied in an effort to reduce swelling to any area. They cause some accumulation of moisture on the surface of the limb after they are applied. To apply a sweat wrap, some sort of medication is applied to the horse's skin, then covered with a layer of plastic kitchen wrap, then bandaged.

Many types of medications are applied to horse limbs via sweat wraps. Glycerin, alcohol, nitrofurazone ointment, DMSO and various cortico- steroid preparations are frequently used alone or in combination. It's hoped that by wrapping the leg in plastic, the leg will be coaxed into "sweating out" excess fluid and the medication that is applied will be "forced" into the leg.

There have really been no studies done on the effectiveness of sweat wraps for treating tendon and ligament injuries. They are generally used at the discretion of the person prescribing treatment for the horse's injury and in accordance with the experience of that person. In the author's experience, most people do not recommend applying a sweat wrap to a tendon or ligament injury in the first few days after the injury has occurred, for fear that they will "heat up" the leg and possibly increase the severity of the injury. However, after a few days have passed, out comes the plastic wrap. Sometimes alternating sweat wraps with cold therapy is advocated. There are really no clear guidelines for the use of sweat wraps in the treatment of tendon and ligament injuries.

Sweat wraps seem to be very popular. In fact, they do seem to be effective at reducing or eliminating minor accumulations of fluid from the lower limbs of the horse. However, what actual effect they have on removing fluid from within injured tendon and ligament tissue and whether they are effective at helping medication penetrate to the site of injury has never actually been evaluated.

Liniments, Poultices and Cataplasms   A mind-boggling array of substances are applied to the horse's skin with the express purpose of increasing heat in the tissue. These chemicals all act as local irritants to the skin. In people, these products cause the blood vessels near the surface of the skin to dilate and the skin to become red. This causes a sensation of warmth on people's skin. (These products also purport to increase or stimulate the circulation to the injured area; more on that later in this chapter.) The effectiveness of liniments and other mild agents that irritate the surface of the skin to produce a therapeutic effect in underlying tendons or ligaments has never been studied in the horse.

Therapeutic Ultrasound   Therapeutic ultrasound is one way of generating heat in tissue. The use of therapeutic ultrasound is discussed in chapter 11.

Hydrotherapy

When a horse's leg is swollen, massaging it with water is one of the first things that people usually do. Water movement and pressure on a limb would seem to be a reasonable way to encourage fluid movement out of a leg. Water pressure massages the injured leg and helps remove the excess fluid from the tissue. There are several ways that hydrotherapy can be done for a horse.

The easiest method of hydrotherapy is to run a hose on the injured leg. Firm water pressure from a hose can be directed at an injured area several times a day for periods of at least thirty minutes. When possible, the temperature of the water can be varied to provide hot or cold effects, as desired. Of course, the problem with this kind of therapy is that it's intensely boring for both the horse and the person doing the treatment and it takes a lot of time and commitment.

Other, less labor-intensive methods of hydrotherapy have thus been developed for horses. "Turbolator" boots are long boots that can be filled with hot or cold water. The horse stands in the boot (hopefully) and air is blown through the water via a small compressor attached to the boot. It's like a miniature Jacuzzi bath for the leg. Larger, more elaborate devices such as water treadmills or whirlpools are also available to do the same sort of thing. Such devices really are quite impressive (and expensive!).

Bandaging

As discussed in chapter 5, bandaging is an effective way of helping to prevent and control fluid accumulation in an injured tendon or ligament. Pressure bandaging should be continued until such time as the swelling in the affected limb is under control.

Exercise

Controlled, early exercise offers many benefits, including helping to stimulate fluid removal from injured tissue. The movement of the leg itself acts like a mechanical pump to help keep fluid moving. Once the fluid accumulation seen in early inflammation is stopped, handwalking the horse can begin. It's not a good idea to let the horse run around freely, however, because he'll most likely just do more damage to his leg.

"Stimulation of Circulation"

The concept of increasing, stimulating or improving circulation to injured areas is a seductive one. After all, there's no question that blood circulation is needed for healing to occur. Blood brings needed oxygen to healing tissue and the circulatory system helps to remove excess tissue fluid and inflammatory by-products. Without question, no circulation to an area is bad. In fact, if there's no circulation to an area, the area just dies and falls off.

It's important to define what is meant by "increasing" circulation. If the idea is to make sure that there is movement of the circulation through a horse's limb, then it's likely that a number of forms of therapy can do this. Such things as massage, mild exercise and hydrotherapy may all be ways in which the movement of fluid can be encouraged from an injured area.

However, if by "increasing" circulation you mean increasing the actual amount of blood that flows to a limb, that's another thing entirely. It's not at all clear that increasing, improving or "stimulating" the amount of circulation to a limb in this way is beneficial, or even possible. No one has ever demonstrated a positive effect on healing of tissue by "increasing" the amount of blood that gets to it. In fact, there are some inflammatory conditions in people in which too many blood vessels in an area is a big part of the problem!

Nevertheless, stimulating or increasing circulation to a previously injured and healing area seems to be a big goal of many people who treat tendon and ligament injuries in horses. Most therapies that are considered for rehabilitating tendon or ligament injury purport to somehow have a positive effect on the circulation. It's just that no one really knows if increasing the circulation is a goal that can be attained or, if it could, if it really makes any difference in healing. Be that as it may, any one of a number of methods are prescribed to increase the circulation in a horse's leg.

Exercise

In addition to its beneficial effects on fluid movement, some veterinarians theorize that another of the benefits of early, controlled exercise is that it stimulates the circulation in the limb. If it does so, it's probably due to an increase in the rate that the heart beats as a result of the exercise.

Liniments

The effects of liniments in increasing heat in tissue were discussed earlier. Some people also believe that liniments increase or improve circulation. Other, more severe methods of irritating the skin, such as blistering, have been advocated for the same purpose and have been shown to be ineffective in affecting the underlying circulation (see below). It seems unlikely that milder forms of the same treatment would be effective. Liniments are unlikely to have any harmful effects on healing tendon and ligament injuries; they're unlikely to do much good, either.

Blistering

Blistering an injured tendon or ligament refers to the application of caustic chemicals, such as red mercury or phenol, to the skin surface overlying the tendon or ligament injury. It's a "treatment" that has literally been around for hundreds of years.

Application of blistering agents to the horse's leg causes the leg to swell up to several times its normal size. Blistering causes tremendous irritation to the skin of the horse's leg. A horse that has been exposed to this procedure needs to be rested until the irritation and swelling subside.

Of course, the proponents of blistering usually describe the "benefits" of treatment as a way to stimulate or improve the circulation. However, blistering has not been demonstrated to be able to affect the circulation to the underlying tendons and ligaments at all.

What blistering does do is enforce rest. When you apply these chemicals to the horse's leg, the leg swells and the skin cracks. The skin can bleed or leak blood serum. Horses that have had their legs blistered are in a lot of pain. They have to rest because their legs are too swollen and sore for them to do anything else. If the only way that you can figure out how to rest your horse is to hurt him, you should be ashamed of yourself. Blistering as therapy has been condemned by the American Humane Society.

Firing

Firing is another archaic treatment for tendon and ligament injuries that has been used for centuries. Firing refers to the application of a hot iron to the skin of the horse. Various decorative patterns of holes are burned through the horse's skin and sometimes into the underlying tendon or ligament tissue.

As with blistering, those who promote firing as a form of therapy talk about its benefits to the circulation of the injured tissue. Still others say that by burning through the skin and into the injured area, any fluid that may be in the area can be released, allowing for healing of the tissue to occur (the same theory is used to describe the benefits of some types of tendon surgery). Some people also say that firing promotes a stabilizing layer of scar tissue around the horse's leg that might act like a physiologic "cast" on the leg to protect it from further injury.

Why firing persists as a treatment in equine medicine defies understanding. Studies have conclusively demonstrated that firing does nothing to the circulation in the underlying tissue. The only thing that firing does is promote the formation of scar tissue in the skin. As you know, scar tissue is weaker, not stronger, than normal tissue. Firing injures the horse and causes him pain. It makes the horse rest. He hurts so much after "treatment" that he can't do anything else.

In spite of the medical literature demonstrating that firing does nothing to help the injured horse, there are still some veterinarians who apparently feel that it is a valuable therapy. In addition, there is a lot of pressure put on veterinarians who work with horses, particularly racehorses, to do it. This pressure comes from owners and trainers who grew up with the procedure and are convinced of its value. Their great-grandfather did it and they are bound and determined to do it, too. (Curiously, in spite of the fact that their great-grandfathers received archaic treatments, too, these same people probably don't look favorably on bleeding or the application of leeches as methods of therapy for themselves.) Some veterinarians truly fear that if they don't fire the horse when asked, they will lose business (and if they don't do it, someone else will). The poor horse is really the only one that must suffer for this nonsense. In the author's opinion, there is no place in modern equine medicine for firing a horse's legs.

Alternative Treatment Options

Just about every alternative method of treating tendon and ligament injuries purports to stimulate or increase the circulation. Some of these treatments are discussed in chapter 11.

Strengthening of Healing Tissue

After you've done what you can to control the inflammatory process and remove fluid from the injured tendon or ligament, your goal in treating your horse is to produce the strongest and most functional tendon possible. To some extent, the horse's body is going to do what it wants to do. You won't be able to affect the outcome of the injury precisely. However, you can help make sure that the outcome is the best that it can be.

It has been well demonstrated that optimum healing of injured tendon and ligament tissue occurs under mild stress. Mechanical stress applied to a leg in the form of mild exercise has been shown to help the healing scar tissue line itself up in a more normal, parallel fashion, similar to what is seen in the uninjured tissue. Therefore, almost everyone now agrees that closely controlled exercise should be resumed early in the post-injury phase for the horse recovering from a tendon or ligament injury.

The precise exercise schedule that is needed for your injured horse is impossible to say here. Designing a rehabilitation schedule is as much an art as it is a science. Each rehabilitation schedule varies, depending on the severity of the initial injury and the response to treatment. Some general principles can be followed, however.

Although no specific studies have been done, most veterinarians think that, after it is injured, tendon or ligament tissue doesn't act all that differently from the other tissues in the horse's body. Therefore, veterinarians assume that the scar tissue forming in the healing tendon will reach 50 percent of its eventual strength in two months. Thus, only very light exercise, such as handwalking, walking on a hot walker, or turnout in a very small space should be allowed in the first two months after injury.

After the first two months, the exercise load should be gradually increased. There are several methods by which this can be done.

The easiest and most obvious way is to slowly add increasing levels of exercise to the horse's rehabilitation program. Initially, the horse can be saddled and walked. (By the way, be careful when you are getting on your well-rested horse for the first time in a couple of months. He may be so happy to see you that he'll buck you off. A bit of tranquilization therapy may well be appropriate to help you both out.) Over the weeks and months that follow, the duration and the intensity of the exercise are gradually increased.

It's very important that you carefully monitor your horse during his rehabilitation. It's not at all uncommon for there to be episodes of minor inflammation in and around the tendon as the rehabilitation process proceeds. For example, as the horse heals, small scar-tissue adhesions that form during the healing process may be stretched and occasionally torn as the tendon regains its full range of motion. This stretching and tearing can create small, local areas of inflammation. You don't want these areas to spread and involve the healing tendon. Thus, if signs of inflammation begin during the rehabilitation process, you need to back off the exercise program until the inflammation subsides.

Repeat ultrasound examinations are particularly useful in monitoring the horse's progress and in making sure that further injury to the healing tissue is not occurring as a result of the rehabilitation process. The tendon or ligament should be examined frequently to make sure that the clinical signs of inflammation are not returning.

As discussed in chapter 3, once the ultrasound examination is normal, it does not mean that the horse is ready to go back to full work. Experience has shown that it may take up to two months after an ultrasound examination shows that the tissue has healed before the horse can be returned to full work. Depending on the severity of the injury, a return to full function may take many months, even as long as a year.

Other forms of exercise, such as swimming or underwater treadmills, have been advocated for rehabilitation of tendon and ligament injuries. They're not bad treatments at all, if you can find a place that has the facilities. The benefits of this sort of therapy come from the fact that water provides resistance to movement in any direction. At the same time, the water cushions and prevents any weight-bearing on the healing leg. Thus, the tissue can be strengthened without impact.

Unfortunately, the problem with swimming injured horses is that the tissue doesn't receive a normal, weight-bearing load while it's being used. In a swimming pool, there's no normal stress put on the horse's leg to encourage the cells of the healing scar tissue to line themselves up in a parallel fashion. A horse is not ready to go back to work right out of the pool. This problem can be overcome by combining swimming exercise with some sort of land-based exercise program.

PROGNOSIS FOR RECOVERY

No matter how carefully you follow your horse in the post-injury period, you will never be able to get an injured tendon or ligament to be as strong as it was before the injury occurred. It may be strong enough for the horse to work, however. The chance of your horse returning to his pre-injury level of exercise depends on several factors, including which structure was injured, how badly it was injured and what exercise level is desired for the horse after he returns from his injury. Some general observations can be made:

- Injuries that involve fractures generally do worse than those that are uncomplicated by broken bones.

- Horses that are expected to perform rigorous athletic functions, such as racing, endurance and jumping, generally have a more difficult time coming back from tendon and ligament injuries than do pleasure horses or horses that do not work hard.
- The more severe the injury to a tendon or ligament, the less likely it is that the horse will be able to work hard once he recovers.
- If a horse has suffered a tendon or ligament injury in the past, when someone else owned him, you can't be sure of how the exercise level that you are going to ask of him is going to affect him in the future. If you are planning on maintaining or reducing his current level of exercise, the horse will probably be fine. If that same horse with a previous injury is coming off an extended lay-up, make sure he's been working regularly before you consider owning him yourself.

Whatever method of therapy and rehabilitation you and your veterinarian select for your horse, adequate time to heal still remains the single most important factor for a successful recovery. Time passes slowly. You will want to ride sooner than you will be able to. Patience on your part is one final factor that will help your horse have a successful recovery from his injury.

CHAPTER 7

Surgical Treatment of Injuries

UNQUESTIONABLY, WHEN A TENDON OR LIGAMENT injury is first suspected, various medical treatments need to be employed to reduce pain, swelling and inflammation. Additionally, however, veterinarians have looked to various surgical methods in an effort to improve healing time, tissue strength and the likelihood of recovery. Depending on the tendon or ligament injury that your horse has suffered, one or more of the following surgical techniques may be applicable.

TENDON SPLITTING OR STABBING

Tendon splitting or stabbing is probably the most commonly performed surgical technique used to treat injured tendons. The technique is also occasionally used to treat injured suspensory ligaments. Tendon splitting was first introduced in the late sixties and it's had something of a recent rebirth after falling into disuse for a while in the mid-seventies and eighties. (The popularity of surgery, like most other things, seems to wax and wane.)

· FIGURE 6 ·

In the standing horse, a scalpel blade can be introduced into an injured tendon in an effort to release fluid from the injured core of the tendon. This is a so-called tendon splitting operation.

Tendon splitting surgery is really quite simple in concept and execution. The surgery is usually done with the horse standing, although some veterinarians prefer to use general anesthesia. When the surgery is performed on the standing horse, the horse's leg is anesthetized (of course) and a scalpel blade is placed through the skin and into the injured portion of the tendon. The scalpel blade is placed parallel to the tendon fibers (perpendicular to the ground) so as to avoid cutting across tendon fibers and creating more damage. Some veterinarians "fan" the scalpel blade around in the area of the tendon that's being treated; others just poke a hole in the tendon at the selected area. Some surgeons also prefer to do the surgery while looking at the tendon with ultrasound in an effort to be as precise as possible in the placement of the scalpel blade (there's absolutely no reason to cut into healthy tendons).

When the surgery was first introduced, the doctors who developed it theorized that it was effective because the hole created by the penetration of the scalpel blade served as an entry point for blood vessels to penetrate the injured area. The blood vessels, they thought, would improve or increase the healing of the injured tendon. However, it was later demonstrated that surgically splitting a tendon was actually harmful when it was done later in the repair process. Some veterinarians also felt that the harm done to the tendon by cutting it with a scalpel blade far outweighed any potential benefit that could be obtained. Therefore, for a while, tendon splitting fell out of favor.

More recently, though, a new theory has been advanced and the surgery has become more popular again (these things really do run in cycles). The new theory of why tendons should be surgically split is that the bleeding and fluid edema that occurs within the tendon as a result of injury needs to be released before the best healing can occur. According to this theory, fluid in a tendon can be compared to fluid inside an abscess. The fluid has to be let out so that healing can occur. As you know, the removal of fluid from an injured tendon or ligament is one of the goals of therapy after the initial inflammation has been controlled. In a tendon or ligament, if the fluid is let out through holes made by a scalpel, the fibers can collapse back together and begin to heal more rapidly. In addition, if blood vessels do get in through the channels created by the scalpel blade, that might be beneficial, too.

Several studies done in 1992 confirmed the benefits of tendon splitting in selected cases. Two clinical studies, done on horses that had sustained injuries while racing or training, demonstrated that tendon splitting led to a significant decrease in the size of the tendon lesion within eight to twelve days after surgery. (These results were also reproduced in horses under experimental conditions.) In addition, the tendons that were treated with tendon splitting in the experimental study had better tissue repair and earlier ingrowth of blood vessels into the tendons than did nonsurgically treated horses.

Surgical splitting should not be used in all tendon and ligament injuries, however. It appears to be most useful in conditions where there is a "core" of fluid within the injured tendon or ligament (remember the jelly doughnut analogy?). In fact, one of the studies mentioned above showed no benefit of tendon splitting in injuries that did not have a core of fluid. Furthermore, it should only be done early in the course of recovery from an injury. If this type of surgery is performed, it should be done within the first week after injury has occurred. There's no benefit (and there is potential harm) to be had from cutting into a tendon that's already late in the healing process.

Finally, a note of caution before you go out and insist that your horse's tendon be split. Long-term follow-up studies that look at the ultimate strength of tendons or ligaments treated by surgical splitting have not been done. Nobody knows if injured tendon or ligament tissue that has been treated by splitting is ultimately as strong as that which occurs from "natural" healing. Clinical experience suggests, however, that the healing after surgery is strong enough for the horse to get by. Tendon splitting, just like all the other forms of treatment for your horse's tendon or ligament injury, does not guarantee that your horse will ever regain the ability to perform at his previous level.

SUPERIOR CHECK LIGAMENT DESMOTOMY

Desmotomy is the cutting or division of a ligament. Remember the superior check ligament? It's the large ligament just above the horse's knee that is thought to help keep the superficial flexor tendon from stretching too far. In the mid-1980s a theory was developed that suggested that the superior check ligament might actually be part of the problem in horses that had troubles with their superficial flexor tendon. Perhaps, so the theory went, the function of the superior check ligament in preventing stretching of the tendon was actually detrimental in these horses. Perhaps the tendon actually needed to stretch more. Or perhaps, in a healing tendon in which there was abnormal and stiff scar tissue, cutting the supporting check ligament might transfer more of the load placed on the horse's leg onto the superficial flexor muscle. That is, by cutting the spot where the superficial flexor tendon is tied to the back of the leg, the entire muscle-tendon unit would be able to stretch more. This might help relieve some of the strain on the tendon and make a re-injury less likely.

In a study done two years after the surgery was initially proposed, the surgery did appear to provide some benefit. It appeared, at least in the one study, that cutting the superior check ligament increased a horse's chances of getting back to his previous level of competition. It also decreased the chance of re-injury to the superficial flexor tendon when compared with other methods of treatment.

Some veterinarians recommend that both superior check ligaments be cut, if cutting one is being considered. The thought here is that if a horse has one leg that hurts, he may overload his good leg and hurt that one, too. It's hoped that the check ligament surgery would help protect the good leg from injury by allowing the muscle-tendon unit to stretch more. Nobody has studied whether this makes sense or not. As a general rule, "normal" is usually the ideal state for the body.

Some veterinarians even recommend two consecutive check ligament surgeries, separated by a couple of months, on the same leg! This is because after the initial surgery, as healing progresses, fibrous scar tissue will try to heal the area that was cut (the body always tries to heal itself). By cutting the area again, it's hoped that the maximum ability to stretch could be obtained. Most horses don't seem to need two surgeries, however. Although the ligament heals in about sixty days, the healed ligament is a little longer than it was before it was cut.

After check ligament surgery, horses are usually bandaged and rested in the stall for two to three weeks. After that comes a period of hand-walking and slow return to exercise, as would be expected in trying to rehabilitate any tendon or ligament injury.

Like everything else that is done to treat tendon injuries, check ligament surgeries are not the only answer to a horse's superficial flexor tendon problem. A number of factors, including the expense of the surgery and the use level desired for the horse after his injury, should be considered. Still, it may be something to think about if your horse has hurt his superficial flexor tendon or if a previous injury to this tendon has been aggravated after good healing was thought to have occurred.

ANNULAR LIGAMENT DESMOTOMY

Problems with the annular ligament that surrounds the tendons at the level of the fetlock joint are seen occasionally in horses, especially in the forelimbs. As opposed to the other tendons and ligaments in the horse's legs, the annular ligament doesn't stretch very much. As a result, when other structures that run through the area swell up or get inflamed, such as the superficial or deep flexor tendons or the tendon sheath, the annular ligament doesn't really expand. Instead, it can restrict the swelling and movement of the injured tissue.

In this way, the annular ligament can act sort of like a boot on a person's ankle, when the person sprains his or her ankle. A boot doesn't stretch much. An ankle that has been sprained swells. If the swelling is restricted by a surrounding boot, the result is extreme pain (and a potentially dangerous restriction of the circulation, which doesn't happen in horses). The boot on the swollen ankle must be removed.

Not all problems with the annular ligament are secondary to injury to other tissues, however. The annular ligament itself may also become thickened and inflamed. Primary annular ligament problems are not particularly common, but when they do occur, they can be quite debilitating for the affected horse. Nobody is exactly sure what causes these primary annular ligament problems.

Whether the annular ligament problems are primary or secondary, the end result for the horse is the same: There's a restriction in the free movement of the tendons around the horse's fetlock joint. Horses with annular ligament problems are usually lame (often for a long time, because the source of their problem can be hard to recognize). The horses can't stand to have their legs flexed at the fetlock joint and often trot off very lame after a flexion test. Many horses with annular ligament problems resent finger pressure on the back of the fetlock joint. Sometimes there's a very obvious clinical appearance to the injured leg. The lower, injured tendon area may be bowed out above the annular ligament, but at the annular ligament the leg will look narrower; the leg can have kind of a "notched" appearance where the annular ligament starts. Any leg can be affected, although it's most commonly the front legs that have the problem. Many of these horses have a history of having improved with rest but then getting worse once they start back to work. Ultrasound examination also helps in the diagnosis of annular ligament (and underlying tendon or tendon sheath) problems.

The treatment for annular ligament problems is pretty straightforward. It's a surgical technique called an annular ligament desmotomy. In the surgery, the annular ligament is sliced in two with a single cut up the back of the ligament, over the deep flexor tendon. This allows for the pressure over the inflamed tendons to be released. If the ligament itself is the primary problem, surgery will allow it to stretch out and relax.

In many cases, annular ligament surgery can be done standing, with the horse sedated and the leg numb from local anesthetic injections. In other cases, general anesthesia may be required so that the underlying structures can be directly observed. General anesthesia is especially important if there are lots of adhesions in the tendon sheath that lies under the annular ligament. With general anesthesia, the tendon sheath can be opened up and the adhesions removed (unfortunately, sometimes horses with lots of adhesions in their tendon sheaths don't come back to full soundness, even with surgery). Recently, arthroscopic surgery has been successfully performed on horses with this problem. Because arthroscopy causes less surgical trauma than conventional surgery, this technique is potentially very advantageous.

The outlook for recovery for horses after annular ligament surgery is generally pretty good, especially if there aren't a lot of other structures involved (like the tendon sheath). Horses with uncomplicated annular ligament problems can usually go back to work within a few months; more complicated problems may require from six to twelve months for full recovery, if full recovery occurs.

SURGICAL REPAIR OF TRAUMATIC INJURIES

Tendon and ligament injuries caused by trauma are some of the ugliest and most unfortunate wounds seen in the horse. The tendons and ligaments between the fetlock joint and the knee or hock joint are the most commonly involved. Usually an obvious cut over the tendon alerts you to the fact that a tendon or ligament may be involved; upon wound exploration by your veterinarian, the deeper trauma is quickly apparent.

Usually some gait or stance abnormality will be seen in a horse after a tendon or ligament injury. When extensor tendons are lacerated, the horse may have a problem pulling his leg forward and may be observed to knuckle over at the fetlock joint or stumble when he walks. Many horses with extensor tendon lacerations can walk normally if they go slow enough, however.

When flexor tendons are cut, stance abnormalities may be noted. When the superficial flexor tendon is cut, usually the only thing seen is that the fetlock joint gets a little lower (closer to the ground). If both the superficial and deep flexor tendons are cut (at the mid–cannon bone area), the toe will come up off the ground and the fetlock joint will sink even further towards the ground. If the laceration goes through the suspensory ligament as well, the horse can't stand on the leg. If the deep flexor tendon is lacerated at the level of the pastern, the toe may rock up but the fetlock joint doesn't sink. (Any of these injuries can be a big problem because in addition to the tendon laceration, the tendon sheath and the nerves, veins and arteries in the area get cut, too.) Finally, if the tendons get cut above the level of the hock joint in the hind leg (the Achilles' tendon apparatus), the horse's hock will flex and drop, and the leg may not be able to bear any weight at all.

Various methods of surgical repair have been attempted for tendon and ligament lacerations. The surgery may vary depending on the degree of injury and the contamination of the area. Lacerated tendons and ligaments can be sutured back together. Alternatively, some sort of an artificial scaffold, such as carbon fibers, may be placed between the ends of a cut tendon or ligament if tissue has been lost due to injury. No single surgery works for every problem.

Extensor Tendon Lacerations

Extensor tendon lacerations are usually pretty easy to treat in the horse. They have a much better prognosis for full recovery than do most flexor tendon injuries. In fact, extensor tendon injuries usually only require surgery to clean up dirt and debris and to remove any ends of dead tendon that can't heal. You don't have to (and usually can't) sew the ends of a lacerated extensor tendon back together.

Horses with extensor tendon injuries may require bandaging, support wraps or special shoes with toe extensions for a short period of time while the wounds heal. Most horses do great after extensor tendon injuries and heal in a month or two. This is true even after some pretty dramatic injuries, such as cutting of the common digital extensor tendon at the level of the knee. If your horse must cut a tendon, tell him to try to cut an extensor tendon. It will be easier.

Flexor Tendon, Tendon Sheath and Suspensory Ligament Lacerations

Flexor tendon and suspensory ligament cuts are usually serious problems. Fresh, clean lacerations may be fixed by sewing the severed tendon ends back together, although some tendon injuries can heal without surgery. The horses are usually put in some sort of cast for several weeks after surgery while the tissue heals. Tendon wounds that are several days old or very contaminated with dirt and/or bacteria usually can't be sewn back together. These wounds get infected easily and come apart if they are sewn together. Contaminated tendon injuries are usually allowed to heal under the protection of a hard cast only.

If the tendon sheath gets involved in a laceration, the prognosis for recovery goes down. Tendon sheath wounds tend to get infected easily and the infection often does not respond to any sort of treatment. Tendon sheath lacerations can be ultimately crippling to the poor horse. If your horse sustains this sort of injury, you really need to consider the value of the horse, his personal worth to you and the expense of long-term treatment before trying to fix his problem. Whether or not to treat a horse with a tendon sheath injury can be a terribly difficult decision.

Many horses with superficial and deep flexor tendon lacerations can be returned to normal athletic function. (Some horses with superficial flexor tendon injuries alone will heal just fine without surgery.) However, if the suspensory ligament gets involved in a laceration, it can be very difficult to save the horse. There is not much chance that a horse with a lacerated suspensory ligament will return to athletic use. Usually repairs are attempted only on valuable breeding animals. Still, there are some reports of horses with these injuries going back to being useful under saddle.

Horses that cut their Achilles' tendon apparatus just above the hock usually don't do well with treatment. If they do make it, horses that have had these injuries will have a large thickening in the area. Never underestimate the capacity of the horse to heal, however. Some horses with Achilles' injuries have made it back to be riding or breeding animals.

CHAPTER 8

Miscellaneous Problems

INFECTED TENDON SHEATHS

Infections of the tendon sheath of the lower limb can be a big problem for a horse. (There are other tendon sheaths in the leg that can occasionally become infected, but problems with them are not commonly seen.) Tendon sheath infections are usually seriously disabling to the horse. They often result in permanent lameness.

The most common cause of infection of the tendon sheath is a penetrating wound that introduces bacteria into the area. Injections of medications into the tendon sheath can also cause infections. (For this reason, injections into tendon sheaths should only be done by trained people using sterile techniques.) Tendon sheath infections have also been seen as a result of infections carried in the blood. In foals, tendon sheaths running next to infected joints have become infected from an extension of the infection into the sheath.

It's not very hard to recognize that a horse has an infected tendon sheath. Horses with infected tendon sheaths become very lame very quickly. The leg is very painful to the touch. It gets hot and swollen as a result of the extreme inflammation that results from the infection.

If a wound occurs over, into or next to a tendon sheath, it should be treated as an emergency. It's not always obvious that the tendon sheath has been penetrated, especially if the wound occurs low on the pastern. X rays and x-ray contrast agents that can outline the depth of penetration of a wound may be useful in determining whether or not a tendon sheath has been entered. It is critical that you find out immediately, *prior* to an infection becoming established in a tendon sheath.

Horses with tendon sheath wounds must be treated very aggressively with antibiotics. Frequently, some sort of surgical intervention is needed to rinse out the tendon sheath or to allow the infected area to drain. This is done to help make sure that an infection doesn't get trapped within the tendon sheath.

Treatment of long-term infections that have become established in the tendon sheath can be very frustrating, unrewarding and expensive. It may take several months to get rid of a chronic tendon sheath infection and the horse may still have some lameness remaining after treatment is finished. (This is because the infections usually cause scar tissue to form in the tendon sheath. The scar tissue restricts the normal gliding movement of the tendon through the sheath.) Before starting treatment on a horse with a chronic tendon sheath infection, you should take all of these factors into consideration.

Tearing of the Superficial Flexor Tendon from the Point of the Hock

In the hind leg, the superficial flexor tendon runs right over the point of the hock. The bone that forms the point of the hock (and the heel of your ankle, which is the analogous joint in you) is called the calcaneus.

As you might imagine, the tendon in this area doesn't just sit passively on the point of the hock; it's tied down on both sides by strong fibrous tissue attachments that prevent the tendon from slipping off to either side. Rarely (fortunately), one of the fibrous tissue attachments can rupture. This is most commonly caused by some sort of trauma or impact on the point of the hock. Usually it's the inside (medial) attachment that is torn, although the outside attachment can tear, too. When one of the attachments gets torn, it allows the tendon to slip over to the side away from where the tear has occurred. In severe cases of this type of injury, the calcaneus can fracture, too.

When a horse tears one of the fibrous attachments of the superficial flexor tendon, it's easy to recognize. Usually there's a great deal of swelling over the point of the hock and the horse is very lame. As the swelling goes down, you can usually feel that the tendon has slipped over to one side of the hock, and you can usually pop it back in place. As soon as the horse walks, however, the tendon will just snap back over to the side again.

Horses that have torn a fibrous attachment of their superficial flexor tendon in a hind limb generally are not very lame after all the initial inflammation goes away. They are left with a bit of a mechanical problem with the way that the leg works, however. A horse with this injury can't move normally because his tendon keeps popping over to the side.

If an athletic horse is desired after this injury, the only treatment for the condition is surgery. After surgery, most horses with a simple tear of a fibrous tissue attachment heal pretty well. They may have some reduced motion in the hock after healing has occurred, however.

If a horse with this injury is just kept as a pet or is only going to be used for breeding, you don't really need to do surgery. The tendon will stay over on one side of the leg, but it will scar in and be relatively stable. This "natural" healing process will allow a horse to be pain-free in pasture.

If fracture of the calcaneus has occurred in addition to injury to the fibrous attachments, the prognosis for return to athletic function is much poorer than with a simple injury to the soft tissue. Horses with fractures of the calcaneus usually don't make it back as athletes, but they can sometimes be useful pets or breeding animals.

CARPAL CANAL SYNDROME

Carpal canal syndrome (carpal tunnel syndrome) isn't a particularly common cause of lameness in the horse. It's caused by increased pressure on the structures that run through the carpal canal, at the back of the horse's knee. It's virtually the same condition that people get in their wrists (which is the analogous anatomical structure in humans).

A fracture of the accessory carpal bone of the horse's knee is the most common cause of carpal canal syndrome. The accessory carpal bone is a small bone located at the back of the horse's knee. Fractures of this bone tend not to heal very well. They result in scar tissue and calcification in the carpal canal. This reduces the normal diameter of the canal. The reduced diameter of the canal has the effect of pinching all the structures that run through it, such as the blood vessels, nerves and tendons. Other causes of carpal canal syndrome include inflammation of the tendons or the tendon sheath itself.

Horses with carpal canal syndrome usually aren't terribly lame, thus complicating the diagnosis. Their lameness may come and go as well. Sometimes swelling of the carpal sheath area can be noted on the inside (medial) part of the upper knee. Horses with this condition also hate having their knees flexed. They will usually trot off very lame after a flexion test of the knee. The lameness in some horses may improve after local anesthetics are injected into the carpal sheath.

Rest will usually make a horse with carpal canal syndrome better. Injections of anti-inflammatory agents, such as corticosteroids or hyaluronic acid, may also be of some help in reducing inflammation. In simple cases of inflammation of the tendon or carpal canal, rest and/or medication may be enough treatment. But if the carpal canal is narrowed, as described above, rest and medical treatment won't solve the horse's problem. Unfortunately, in a horse with a narrowed carpal canal, as soon as he starts back to work, the lameness usually returns.

The only successful treatment for horses with a narrowed carpal canal is surgery. The pressure in the carpal canal caused by a reduced diameter can be relieved by making a slit in the fibrous sheath. Horses tend to do pretty well after surgery. Like any surgery, however, there can be complications and not all horses will make a successful recovery.

CHRONIC STRAIN INJURIES

In some older horses, poorly conformed horses, heavy horses and pregnant mares (who are temporarily heavy), the tendons and ligaments of the lower limbs can begin to give way. In these unfortunate animals, the stress and strain that is placed on the legs is more than the tissue is able to handle. Over time, the legs of a horse with this problem will begin to stretch downward, causing the fetlock joint to bend to an almost 90 degree angle.

Horses with poor limb conformation seem to have a particularly difficult time with chronic strain injuries (and indeed with many problems of tendons and ligaments). If the horse's pasterns are long and sloping (commonly known as being "coon footed") or if the horse's hocks are straight and lack their normal amount of angle, additional stress is apparently passed onto the tendons and ligaments. If these poorly conformed horses get heavy, injured or old, they seem to have an extremely hard time getting better if tendon and ligament problems occur. Apparently, the stress on the poorly built frame of the horse is just more than the system can bear. That's not to say that all horses with poor conformation will develop chronic strain problems in their tendons and ligaments. It's just that if these horses do develop problems, it can be exceedingly difficult to get them to heal.

The treatment for chronic strain problems is frustrating and unrewarding. Heavy bandages applied to the lower limbs of these horses have been used in an effort to help resist the bending of the fetlock joint. Horseshoes have been devised with a supporting sling to go under the fetlock joint. These may provide some temporary support but pressure sores on the underside of the fetlock joint soon become a problem. Horseshoes with extended heels have been advocated by some people to provide additional "support" to the back of the horse's leg.

In reality, trying to help a horse with chronic strain injuries due to time, weight and/or conformation is a very frustrating process. You're really just swimming against the tide of nature. Although you may be able to help a horse that's "breaking down" with chronic strain in the short run (say, to get an old mare through her pregnancy), over the long haul this condition can't be cured. There's no way to reverse the process. You ultimately may have to just retire an old friend due to a chronic strain condition.

CHAPTER 9

Bandages, Boots and Support Wraps

SOME SORT OF BANDAGE OR BOOT SEEMS TO GET PUT ON a horse's leg for just about any problem, especially those involving tendons or ligaments. Boots and bandages are most commonly applied to the legs of the horse for one of three reasons: to control swelling, for protection and for support.

CONTROLLING SWELLING

First, as discussed in chapter 5, bandages are used to control swelling in an injured limb (boots generally are not used for the control of swelling). Obviously, the pressure from a properly applied bandage can be useful in helping control or contain swelling in a leg that has sustained an injury to a tendon or ligament.

PROTECTION

Second, boots and bandages provide some degree of protection to a limb. Protection of a limb may be desirable during exercise or when a horse is being transported in a trailer. The mere fact that something is hanging on or around the leg of the horse will help provide some protection against trauma. Such trauma frequently comes from the horse himself.

When they move, some horses may hit one leg against the leg on the opposite side (this is called interfering). Interference usually occurs at the level of the fetlock joint. Therefore, boots and bandages used to protect the horse from interfering cover this joint.

Some horses may also step on their front legs with their hind legs (this is called forging). Forging trauma usually occurs to the heels of the front foot. Horses that step on their front heels can peel the skin and hoof right off the back of the heel. In an attempt to prevent this type of wound, called a scalp wound (the horse's shoe acts just like the knife of a frontier scalper), a "bell" boot is commonly applied to the horse's pastern. The boot hangs over the foot and ideally helps protect it from trauma.

Occasionally, forging or interfering injuries can be truly catastrophic to the horse. There is an incredible amount of force generated by the rapidly moving legs of the horse. The force in the front leg moving forward at the canter has been measured at up to seventy-two times the force of gravity! Remember also that attached to the foot is a metal shoe. With that amount of force behind it, a metal shoe can be quite an instrument of destruction. If one leg is accidentally struck or stepped on by another leg, the consequences can be devastating. This is especially so if the horse steps on his front tendons with a back foot. Major disruptions of tendons, ligaments and even bone can occur with this sort of injury. In reality, no boot or bandage can protect a horse from this sort of major trauma.

SUPPORT

The third and most poorly understood function of boots and bandages is in providing "support" to the horse's limb. What is support, anyway?

When a horse's leg hits the ground, all of the force applied to the leg goes straight down (the amount of force relates to the weight of the horse as well as to the speed at which he is travelling). Of course, viewed from the side, the horse's leg isn't straight. There's a bend at the fetlock joint. This means that as the horse moves, the fetlock joint is pushed down into the ground by the force applied to the leg (you must have seen pictures of Thoroughbred racehorses with their fetlock joints buried in the dirt). As the fetlock joint goes lower and lower, the muscles, tendons and ligaments on the back of the leg must stretch to accommodate the force that's being applied to them.

Support bandages or boots try to prevent the downward stretching of the leg at the fetlock joint. They also are supposed to absorb some of the energy transmitted to the horse's leg. In addition, because they are somewhat elastic, when the leg is in the air, support boots and bandages are supposed to help the leg snap back into the position that it was in before the fetlock joint was forced down by the weight of the horse. (In the same manner, a rubber band returns to its "normal" shape after the pressure is released from it.)

Given the frequency with which support boots and bandages are applied to the legs of horses and the zeal with which it is done, surprisingly little study has gone into examining whether or not they actually do anything. It has been fairly well determined that some support is provided to the horse's leg by bandaging (boots have so far not been studied). Beyond that, not much is clear.

To provide any significant support to a limb, a boot or bandage must go down below the level of the fetlock joint to the horse's pastern. This seems rather obvious, doesn't it? If a boot or bandage is wrapped only around the tendons and ligaments above the level of the fetlock joint, the force that is applied to the fetlock joint is pretty much unaffected. It goes right through the middle of the bandage. Stretching of the tendons and ligaments of the leg is not restricted by a boot or bandage that just circles the leg.

The tension that is applied with a boot or bandage affects the amount of support provided to the horse's leg. It appears that the tighter the wrap is applied to the limb, the more support the limb gets. You could make a theoretical argument that a bandage might be better than a boot in providing support, since the bandage can be applied more tightly. (Obviously, there's a limit to how tightly you can apply a bandage without making a tourniquet; this is where experience comes in.) Unfortunately, the support from a tight wrap seems to wear off more quickly than the support provided by a moderately tight bandage. Tight wraps apparently tend to loosen up more quickly than loose ones do. Boots, on the other hand, may not loosen up much at all once they are fastened in place. However, again, nobody has really studied the *actual* effects of "support" boots.

The configuration of a support bandage appears to affect the amount of support that is provided, as well. Most times, support wraps are just wrapped around the leg in one direction or another (contrary to what many people believe, the direction of the wrap doesn't make a bit of difference). To provide maximum support, it appears that a bandage should be applied to the leg in a figure-eight manner in order to support the base of the fetlock joint. A wrap applied in this fashion passes under the fetlock joint and pulls the fetlock joint up slightly. Pulling up on the fetlock joint has the effect of making the joint slightly more upright and helps to reduce the bend at the fetlock joint that occurs from the force on the leg.

"Splints" of bandage material over the back of the limb appear to provide additional support to the horse's tendons and ligaments, as well. A splint is made by applying a few long layers of bandage material directly over the tendons, parallel to the direction of the tendons from the upper tendon area to below the fetlock joint. The support bandage is then applied over the top of the supporting splint.

PROBLEMS WITH BOOTS AND BANDAGES

Boots and bandages are not necessarily benign. It is possible to apply them too tightly, especially bandages. If a bandage is applied with too much tension, it can restrict or cut off the circulation to the underlying skin and limb. Among other things, this may result in the so-called "bandage bow." A leg with a bandage bow will swell and have an appearance that looks just like an acute, severe tendon injury. On ultrasound examination, however, it can be seen that the tendons underneath the swelling have not been harmed. Still, a full recovery from a bandaging injury can take several weeks.

Improperly applied bandages can cause pressure sores and loss of skin on the limb. The formation of pressure sores is a particular problem over the back of the carpus (knee). At this level, the skin overlies the large accessory carpal bone. This area is something of a pressure point. Sores can develop here quite easily and rapidly. Special care and protection must be provided if the horse's knee is to be bandaged. Similar problems are seen with bandages that are applied to the horse's hock. Over time, even areas that are relatively resistant to the formation of pressure sores, such as the back of the tendons, can start to peel and lose skin.

Boots, especially those made from neoprene, are not without their own set of problems. Some horses are allergic to neoprene. After exercise, the leg of a horse with a neoprene allergy may swell dramatically. The irritation to the leg from the neoprene may even cause the leg to leak serum. This gives the appearance of a severe, acute infection.

Finally, both boots and bandages tend to insulate a leg. This at least has the potential for causing heat build-up inside the limb. As you recall from chapter 2, thermal injury is theorized to be one of the causes of tendon and ligament injuries. No one has ever looked at this to see if increased limb heat from a boot or bandage is a real problem, however.

In reality, remarkably little is known about the true effects (beneficial or harmful) of "supporting" a horse's leg with boots and bandages, although it seems as if they should have some positive effect. Even though this hasn't necessarily been proven, there's no reason not to try to help your exercising horse by protecting or supporting his legs. There's also no reason to be dogmatic in your beliefs about the importance of doing so.

CHAPTER 10

Horseshoeing and Its Effects on Tendons and Ligaments

In the horse world, there's a tremendous amount of attention given to the relation between the horse's feet and their tendons and ligaments. When you think about it, the horse's hoof is about the only part of the horse that is easily affected or changed by people. Consequently it gets trimmed and manipulated regularly. Thus, it's probably inevitable that people begin to wonder what, if any, effect changes made to the hoof have on the leg. And it's probably also unavoidable that changes in the horse's hoof get blamed or credited for much of what goes on in the leg above it.

Up until fairly recently there has not been a tremendous amount of investigation into the effects of shoeing on the tendons and ligaments of the horse's leg. Most people figure that changes made to the horse's foot should do *something* to the leg. Just exactly what that something might be becomes a matter of opinion and supposition (people suppose that this change in the foot might have that effect on the tendons or ligaments). As a result of all of this guesswork, a lot of misinformation is lurking out there in the horse world. But much of what is commonly believed by the horse-owning public about the effects of shoeing on the leg has been demonstrated to be untrue by the studies that have been performed.

THE NORMAL FOOT

Briefly, you need some basic information about what's considered normal in the horse's foot. If the bottom of the hoof is level with the ground, the front part of the hoof wall (the toe) forms an angle with the ground. Of course, all angles are measured in degrees. The angle of the normal front foot in most horses is from 50 to 55 degrees (many people think it should be lower than that; they're misinformed). The angle of the normal hind foot is usually a bit steeper, between 53 and 57 degrees.

Individual horses can vary in the angle of their feet and still be normal. However, if a horse's hoof angle is very steep, if the toe is short or if the heel is long, the horse tends towards what is known as a "clubfoot" conformation. Conversely, if the toe is long and the heel is quite short, the horse is said to have an underslung heel.

The proper angle of the hoof for an individual horse is reported by some people to be equal to the angle of the shoulder (this can be seen by drawing a line from the crest of the withers, through the shoulder and to the ground). In reality, the true angle of the shoulder is a bit difficult to measure. Therefore, most people look at an imaginary line extending from the fetlock to the ground. Most people feel that there should be a straight line from the middle of the fetlock through the middle of the hoof when the hoof is viewed from the side and from the front. Indeed there is some scientific evidence to support this idea.

· Figure 7 ·

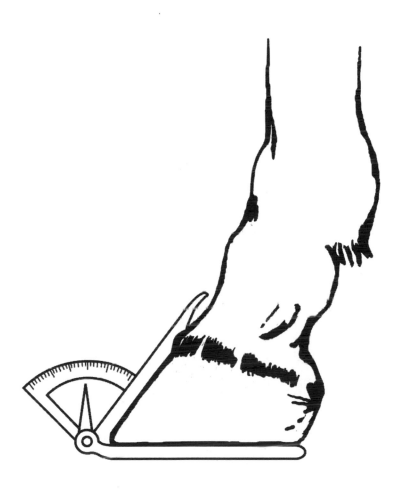

The angle of the horse's foot is generally felt to be important, as it relates to tendon and ligament strain. The true effects of hoof angle on tendons and ligaments are probably not what you think!

The balance of the hoof is also evaluated. Balance refers to the length of the sides of the feet when compared to each other. A balanced foot is the same length on both sides of the hoof when seen from the front or the back. When the foot is picked up, a line drawn from the toe down the middle of the frog should split the hoof down the middle.

Finally, foot length is evaluated. Foot length is measured from the coronary band to the toe.

Things People Think Are True about Horseshoeing and Its Effects on Tendons and Ligaments

So far, no one has actually studied the effects that hoof balance and foot length have on the tendons and ligaments of the horse's lower leg (not that there aren't people out there who will tell you that they know the effects). Most people suppose that a horse that is "out of balance" will land awkwardly and unevenly, putting more stress on one side of the leg or another and leading to injury. Similarly, most people seem to agree that a horse with a foot that is too long may tend to stumble or trip, leading to the possibility of leg injuries. (Horses with short feet tend to get sore in their feet.) It seems hardly controversial to suggest that the horse's foot should be of an appropriate length and in balance, whatever the actual effects these things have on tendons and ligaments.

The hoof angle is another thing entirely. The effects of hoof angle on the tendons and ligaments of the lower leg of the horse have been looked at extensively.

Most people believe that if a horse has a low heel, more strain will be placed on his tendons and ligaments. They reason that if the horse's heel is low, the leg will tend to sink down at the fetlock. If the horse sinks at the fetlock, so the story goes, the tendons and ligaments running down the back of the leg will be stretched more than if the foot is at a normal angle. Conversely, the general belief is that if the heel is elevated, stress and strain on the tendons and ligaments is relieved because the leg doesn't stretch down as much. Consequently, when a horse hurts one of the flexor tendons or the suspensory ligament, one of the most commonly recommended changes to the horse is an elevation in his hoof angle. As you will see, this may not be appropriate.

THE THINGS THAT HAVE ACTUALLY BEEN PROVEN ABOUT HOOF ANGLE AND ITS EFFECTS ON TENDONS AND LIGAMENTS

Many horseshoers and trainers feel that by making the toe longer, it will make the horse stride longer (this has been shown to be untrue). However, most people in the veterinary community feel it's a bad thing for a horse to have a low, undershung heel. There is data that shows that horses with this sort of foot conformation have more foot lameness than do horses with a normal angle. It's also been shown that problems which keep horses from racing or training are significantly higher in horses with low heels than in horses with normal foot angles. It has not, however, been specifically shown that horses with low heels have more tendon and ligament problems than do horses with a more normal hoof angle.

Actually, changes in the angle of the horse's foot appear to have very little effect on the tendons and ligaments. Two studies have measured the strain in the tendons and ligaments of the forelimb when shoeing angle changes were made. Using strain gauges to measure any stress that might occur in the tendons and ligaments, the angle of the foot has been changed from 40 to 70 degrees in one study and from 55 to 78 degrees in another study. Here are the effects of hoof angle changes on the major tendons and ligaments that have been studied:

- *The superficial flexor tendon*   No change in strain was noted with any heel elevation in this tendon, according to one study. In another study, elevation of the heel from 5 to 10 degrees *increased* the strain in the superficial flexor tendon slightly at the trot. (In that same study, elevation of the toe slightly decreased the strain. This suggests that the heels should actually be lowered if a horse hurts his superficial flexor tendon. This is not at all what you'd think. It's really quite confusing, isn't it?)

- *The deep flexor tendon*   With heel elevation, a slight decrease in strain in this tendon was noted. However, there must be a change of about fifteen degrees (that's a tremendous change) for anything significant to be noted. (It actually makes some sense that the strain in the deep flexor tendon can be affected by hoof angle changes, since the deep flexor tendon inserts into the bone of the foot.)

- *The suspensory ligament*   At best, studies have shown that shoeing changes do nothing to the suspensory ligament. However, there have been two studies that have demonstrated that elevating the heels actually increases the strain in the suspensory ligament. This would almost certainly be harmful to a horse trying to recover from a suspensory ligament injury.

What's the bottom line? In reality, it may not make much difference at all if you try to help the horse with an injured tendon or ligament by changing his shoeing. Elevating the heel certainly doesn't appear to be helpful at all. In the case of an injury to the suspensory ligament or the superficial flexor tendon, you may actually make his problem worse by elevating his heel. (In fact, some veterinarians advise *lowering* the heel to treat horses with injured superficial flexor tendons.)

Whatever you do to your horse's foot to "help" him with his tendons and ligaments, make sure that it makes sense. Discuss any proposed changes with your veterinarian and your farrier. In reality, it appears that if you think you can actually do something important for your horse with an injured tendon or ligament by changing his shoeing, you're probably just fooling yourself. In most cases, the best idea is to make sure that each leg is shod with the foot at an appropriate length, angle and balance.

CHAPTER 11

Therapeutic Options

IT'S PROBABLY NATURAL THAT PEOPLE WANT TO DO everything that they can for a horse with a tendon or ligament injury. Frankly, the treatment that can be provided by the veterinary community for these injuries is somewhat anticlimactic and disappointing. Treatment requires a lot of time and results in tissue that is ultimately somewhat weaker than normal. At this point, that's the best that can be done. Traditional veterinary treatment is not very exciting and it's not effective at returning the tendon to its pre-injured, "normal" state. That goal appears, at least at this time, to be impossible.

Some people are unwilling to accept the inherent limitations in the healing process and the seemingly slow pace of veterinary research, however. Therefore, they turn to other, nontraditional methods of therapy in an effort to speed up or otherwise "improve" the healing process. What these methods have in common are (1) limited, if any, research into their effectiveness; (2) glowing claims as to how well they work and (3) someone who's willing to sell them to you.

Veterinarians are not unwilling to accept alternative, nontraditional therapies, by the way. Everyone wants to help an injured horse. What veterinarians want is proof that a treatment works before recommending it (as any good scientist should). The fact that someone says something is great does not mean that it is. It's healthy to be a little skeptical. That's why so many veterinarians have a wait-and-see attitude towards nontraditional or alternative therapies. They don't want to dismiss a potentially useful therapy, but they don't want to embrace an unproven, futile therapeutic effort with open arms, either. Who knows, someday one of these therapies might be demonstrated to actually do something.

You should have some idea about what people will tell you can be done to "help" your horse with an injured tendon or ligament to heal, if only to protect yourself from aggressive salespeople. The feeling that you want to do everything you can for your horse is a good one; don't let someone take advantage of it.

LASERS

"Soft" lasers (also known as "cold" lasers), laser light of less energy than that used to cut tissue, have been used to treat a number of conditions of the horse's musculoskeletal system. This type of treatment uses low-level light energy in an effort to produce certain effects in the tissue. Proponents of laser therapy say the laser light stimulates cell metabolism and improves healing by improving blood flow (the universal goal of alternative therapies), enhancing protein formation and relieving pain, among other things. How it might do so isn't known, however. Actually, laser therapy has fallen out of favor in recent years.

Two studies have been done on horses; neither showed any significant effect of laser therapy on the treatment of tendinitis. Nor have studies shown any beneficial effects of laser therapy on treating healing wounds in horses (another area where they are commonly used). At this point, laser therapy can best be described as something you can do to a horse that has had a tendon or ligament injury. What, if anything, you are doing is another question.

THERAPEUTIC ULTRASOUND

As you know, high-frequency sound waves, known as ultrasound, are indispensable in making accurate diagnoses of tendon and ligament injuries. What you may not know is that ultrasound also can be used as a form of therapy. Therapeutic ultrasound has been used for many years in physical therapy in people. It has been used to a much lesser extent in animals, however. Interestingly, the actual effects of ultrasound on tissue haven't been studied very much. Still, there are many applications for this technology in people.

The ultrasonic sound waves that penetrate tissue create heat. A number of benefits of ultrasound have been reported in people, including improved healing, reduction of scar tissue and stimulation of collagen production.

The problem with the use of therapeutic ultrasound is that there has been very limited study of its effects on healing tendons and ligaments in the horse. Those studies that have been done are somewhat contradictory; some show that there is improved healing but others show no effect whatsoever. Although the heat produced by ultrasound might help move fluid out of injured tissue, ultrasound certainly has the potential to retard healing, too. If you start heating up an acutely inflamed tendon or ligament, there's certainly the potential to increase the damage. If you caused heat damage in an acutely injured tendon or ligament, you could conceivably increase swelling or bleeding of the injured tissue. There are no standard dosages or treatment regimens that can be followed if you want to try this form of therapy on your horse. Ultrasound is an instance where the machines are out there, but no one really knows if or how well they work. Don't expect miracles.

ELECTROMAGNETIC THERAPY

There is starting to be some evidence that the application of electromagnetic energy to tissue can occasionally do something to tissue. That is, if you apply electromagnetic energy to tissue, you will sometimes see some effect. Unfortunately, you can't predict what that effect will be. Sometimes the effect is negative. Like ultrasound, electromagnetic therapy is another therapy that can be applied even though nobody really knows what, if anything, they are actually doing.

Electromagnetic therapy has shown some occasional benefit in treating fractured bones that don't heal properly (nonunion fractures). Studies in rabbit tendons have suggested that electromagnetic therapy may help promote the formation of collagen and also helps it to find a parallel fiber arrangement more rapidly. Healed, surgically cut tendons and ligaments in rats and rabbits, respectively, were found to be stronger after electromagnetic therapy had been applied.

Once again, though, studies in horses are lacking. Electromagnetic therapy did not increase or improve wound healing in one study. In another, electromagnetic therapy actually made surgically created superficial flexor tendon defects worse. Although there might eventually be some place for electromagnetic therapy in the treatment of tendon and ligament injuries in the horse, there's not enough evidence to support its use or necessity in treating these problems now.

MAGNETIC THERAPY

Many people are buying magnetic boots to put on their horse's legs. According to one manufacturer, magnetic boots, pads and wraps are something of a cure-all for horse problems. One manufacturer states that these magnetic devices improve healing of a variety of conditions by "improving" circulation (again). The company even paid for a study to be done that concluded that the magnetic boots increased the circulation in the limbs that they were applied to.

In fact, no one knows what, if any, effect these marvelous magnetic miracle makers have on horse limbs. Once again, the ability to make something has outpaced the ability to see if that something actually works. There seems to be little likelihood that magnetic boots could hurt a horse; there seems to be equally little likelihood that they could be of significant help, as well. There's little harm in trying such devices on your horse. There's little reason to believe, at least at this point, that they are of any significant benefit, either.

ACUPUNCTURE

The benefits of acupuncture on healing tendon and ligament injuries in horses have not been documented. Acupuncture is a departure from traditional Western medicine. An understanding of acupuncture is achieved only after much study, and a discussion of its purported benefits is beyond the scope of this book. Acupuncture has been shown to have some effects in the relief of some painful conditions of horses, particularly of the horse's back. What, if any, benefit can be obtained by treating a horse's tendon or ligament injury with acupuncture is anybody's guess. Presumably, some relief from the pain of an injury would be welcomed by the injured horse.

Alternative therapies for tendon and ligament injuries persist because of the limitations of traditional medicine and the problems with normal healing. Fortunately, none of the alternative therapies discussed in this chapter appear to be consistently harmful to the horse. It's just that glowing reports of their effectiveness can't be supported by any medical facts. Just because a trainer is paid to endorse a particular product doesn't mean that the trainer has the medical knowledge to assess the actual benefits of a particular treatment (if, in fact, such benefits exist).

The veterinary community is continuously studying and evaluating all forms of treatment for injured tendons and ligaments, including alternative therapies. Everyone wants the injured horse to get better. Just because you want to do something, don't resort to doing just anything.

EPILOGUE

Believe it or not, research has demonstrated that people tend to believe anything they are told. Everyone knows that tendon and ligament injuries are bad things in horses. Everyone would like to do whatever is possible to make the injured horse better. Every expert, legitimate or otherwise, will tell you *something*.

The state of the art of tendon and ligament healing isn't very advanced in horses. Some of this is due to a lack of study, although as studies are done, it becomes increasingly apparent that tendons and ligaments may not have the capacity to heal in the same fashion as other tissues. Therefore, ideal healing and rehabilitation of these types of injuries may just be a type of damage control.

Each horse's tendon and ligament injury is different and may need to be handled in a slightly different way. The only constant in dealing with tendon and ligament injuries is that healing will take a lot of time and patience. Proper medical care should be directed by your veterinarian. The horse will heal as fast as he can. Making sure everything gets taken care of in a proper and reasonable fashion is up to you.

BIBLIOGRAPHY

Balch, O. M., et al. "Hoof Balance and Lameness: Improper Toe Length, Hoof Angle and Mediolateral Balance." *Compendium on Continuing Education* 17, no. 10 (1995): 1275–83.

Dyson, S., ed. "Tendon and Ligament Injuries, Vol. I." *The Veterinary Clinics of North America, Equine Practice* 9, no. 3 (August 1994).

———. "Tendon and Ligament Injuries, Vol. 2." *The Veterinary Clinics of North America, Equine Practice* 11, no. 2 (August 1995).

Getty, R.T. *Sisson and Grossman's The Anatomy of the Domestic Animals,* 5th ed. Philadelphia: W. B. Saunders Company, 1975.

Jones, W. E. *Equine Sports Medicine.* Philadelphia: Lea and Febiger, 1989.

Robinson, N. E., ed. *Current Therapy in Equine Medicine,* 3rd ed. Philadelphia: W. B. Saunders Company, 1992.

White, N. A., and J. N. Moore. *Current Practice of Equine Surgery.* Philadelphia: J. B. Lippincott and Company, 1990.

INDEX